C-1327   CAREER EXAMINATION SERIES

*This is your
PASSBOOK for...*

Cashier/ Cashier I

*Test Preparation Study Guide
Questions & Answers*

COPYRIGHT NOTICE

This book is SOLELY intended for, is sold ONLY to, and its use is RESTRICTED to individual, bona fide applicants or candidates who qualify by virtue of having seriously filed applications for appropriate license, certificate, professional and/or promotional advancement, higher school matriculation, scholarship, or other legitimate requirements of education and/or governmental authorities.

This book is NOT intended for use, class instruction, tutoring, training, duplication, copying, reprinting, excerption, or adaptation, etc., by:

1) Other publishers
2) Proprietors and/or Instructors of "Coaching" and/or Preparatory Courses
3) Personnel and/or Training Divisions of commercial, industrial, and governmental organizations
4) Schools, colleges, or universities and/or their departments and staffs, including teachers and other personnel
5) Testing Agencies or Bureaus
6) Study groups which seek by the purchase of a single volume to copy and/or duplicate and/or adapt this material for use by the group as a whole without having purchased individual volumes for each of the members of the group
7) Et al.

Such persons would be in violation of appropriate Federal and State statutes.

PROVISION OF LICENSING AGREEMENTS – Recognized educational, commercial, industrial, and governmental institutions and organizations, and others legitimately engaged in educational pursuits, including training, testing, and measurement activities, may address request for a licensing agreement to the copyright owners, who will determine whether, and under what conditions, including fees and charges, the materials in this book may be used them. In other words, a licensing facility exists for the legitimate use of the material in this book on other than an individual basis. However, it is asseverated and affirmed here that the material in this book CANNOT be used without the receipt of the express permission of such a licensing agreement from the Publishers. Inquiries re licensing should be addressed to the company, attention rights and permissions department.

All rights reserved, including the right of reproduction in whole or in part, in any form or by any means, electronic or mechanical, including photocopying, recording, or by any information storage and retrieval system, without permission in writing from the Publisher.

Copyright © 2024 by
National Learning Corporation

212 Michael Drive, Syosset, NY 11791
(516) 921-8888 • www.passbooks.com
E-mail: info@passbooks.com

PUBLISHED IN THE UNITED STATES OF AMERICA

PASSBOOK® SERIES

THE *PASSBOOK® SERIES* has been created to prepare applicants and candidates for the ultimate academic battlefield – the examination room.

At some time in our lives, each and every one of us may be required to take an examination – for validation, matriculation, admission, qualification, registration, certification, or licensure.

Based on the assumption that every applicant or candidate has met the basic formal educational standards, has taken the required number of courses, and read the necessary texts, the *PASSBOOK® SERIES* furnishes the one special preparation which may assure passing with confidence, instead of failing with insecurity. Examination questions – together with answers – are furnished as the basic vehicle for study so that the mysteries of the examination and its compounding difficulties may be eliminated or diminished by a sure method.

This book is meant to help you pass your examination provided that you qualify and are serious in your objective.

The entire field is reviewed through the huge store of content information which is succinctly presented through a provocative and challenging approach – the question-and-answer method.

A climate of success is established by furnishing the correct answers at the end of each test.

You soon learn to recognize types of questions, forms of questions, and patterns of questioning. You may even begin to anticipate expected outcomes.

You perceive that many questions are repeated or adapted so that you can gain acute insights, which may enable you to score many sure points.

You learn how to confront new questions, or types of questions, and to attack them confidently and work out the correct answers.

You note objectives and emphases, and recognize pitfalls and dangers, so that you may make positive educational adjustments.

Moreover, you are kept fully informed in relation to new concepts, methods, practices, and directions in the field.

You discover that you are actually taking the examination all the time: you are preparing for the examination by "taking" an examination, not by reading extraneous and/or supererogatory textbooks.

In short, this PASSBOOK®, used directedly, should be an important factor in helping you to pass your test.

CASHIER/CASHIER I

DUTIES:
   Receives, records, and deposits daily cash receipts at an institution or department; performs related duties as required.

SUBJECT OF EXAMINATION:
The written test is designed to evaluate knowledge, skills and /or abilities in the following areas:
1. **Cashiering Principles and Practices** - These questions are designed to test for an understanding of such things as proper cashiering practices; terminology; and cashiering issues pertaining to currency, checks and other negotiable instruments.
2. **Clerical operations with letters and numbers** - These questions test for skills and abilities in clerical operations involving alphabetizing, comparing, checking and counting. The questions require you to follow the specific directions given for each question which may involve alphabetizing, comparing, checking and counting given groups of letters and/or numbers.
3. **Name and number checking** - These questions test for the ability to distinguish between sets of words, letters, and/or numbers that are almost exactly alike. Material is usually presented in two or three columns, and you will have to determine how the entry in the first column compares with the entry in the second column and possibly the third. You will be instructed to mark your answers according to a designated code provided in the directions.
4. **Public contact principles and practices** - These questions test for the ability to interact with other people, to gather and present information, and to provide assistance, advice, and effective customer service in a courteous and professional manner. Questions will cover such topics as understanding and responding to people with diverse needs, perspectives, personalities, and levels of familiarity with agency operations, as well as acting in a way that both serves the public and reflects well on your agency.

HOW TO TAKE A TEST

I. YOU MUST PASS AN EXAMINATION

A. WHAT EVERY CANDIDATE SHOULD KNOW

Examination applicants often ask us for help in preparing for the written test. What can I study in advance? What kinds of questions will be asked? How will the test be given? How will the papers be graded?

As an applicant for a civil service examination, you may be wondering about some of these things. Our purpose here is to suggest effective methods of advance study and to describe civil service examinations.

Your chances for success on this examination can be increased if you know how to prepare. Those "pre-examination jitters" can be reduced if you know what to expect. You can even experience an adventure in good citizenship if you know why civil service exams are given.

B. WHY ARE CIVIL SERVICE EXAMINATIONS GIVEN?

Civil service examinations are important to you in two ways. As a citizen, you want public jobs filled by employees who know how to do their work. As a job seeker, you want a fair chance to compete for that job on an equal footing with other candidates. The best-known means of accomplishing this two-fold goal is the competitive examination.

Exams are widely publicized throughout the nation. They may be administered for jobs in federal, state, city, municipal, town or village governments or agencies.

Any citizen may apply, with some limitations, such as the age or residence of applicants. Your experience and education may be reviewed to see whether you meet the requirements for the particular examination. When these requirements exist, they are reasonable and applied consistently to all applicants. Thus, a competitive examination may cause you some uneasiness now, but it is your privilege and safeguard.

C. HOW ARE CIVIL SERVICE EXAMS DEVELOPED?

Examinations are carefully written by trained technicians who are specialists in the field known as "psychological measurement," in consultation with recognized authorities in the field of work that the test will cover. These experts recommend the subject matter areas or skills to be tested; only those knowledges or skills important to your success on the job are included. The most reliable books and source materials available are used as references. Together, the experts and technicians judge the difficulty level of the questions.

Test technicians know how to phrase questions so that the problem is clearly stated. Their ethics do not permit "trick" or "catch" questions. Questions may have been tried out on sample groups, or subjected to statistical analysis, to determine their usefulness.

Written tests are often used in combination with performance tests, ratings of training and experience, and oral interviews. All of these measures combine to form the best-known means of finding the right person for the right job.

II. HOW TO PASS THE WRITTEN TEST

A. NATURE OF THE EXAMINATION

To prepare intelligently for civil service examinations, you should know how they differ from school examinations you have taken. In school you were assigned certain definite pages to read or subjects to cover. The examination questions were quite detailed and usually emphasized memory. Civil service exams, on the other hand, try to discover your present ability to perform the duties of a position, plus your potentiality to learn these duties. In other words, a civil service exam attempts to predict how successful you will be. Questions cover such a broad area that they cannot be as minute and detailed as school exam questions.

In the public service similar kinds of work, or positions, are grouped together in one "class." This process is known as *position-classification*. All the positions in a class are paid according to the salary range for that class. One class title covers all of these positions, and they are all tested by the same examination.

B. FOUR BASIC STEPS

1) Study the announcement

How, then, can you know what subjects to study? Our best answer is: "Learn as much as possible about the class of positions for which you've applied." The exam will test the knowledge, skills and abilities needed to do the work.

Your most valuable source of information about the position you want is the official exam announcement. This announcement lists the training and experience qualifications. Check these standards and apply only if you come reasonably close to meeting them.

The brief description of the position in the examination announcement offers some clues to the subjects which will be tested. Think about the job itself. Review the duties in your mind. Can you perform them, or are there some in which you are rusty? Fill in the blank spots in your preparation.

Many jurisdictions preview the written test in the exam announcement by including a section called "Knowledge and Abilities Required," "Scope of the Examination," or some similar heading. Here you will find out specifically what fields will be tested.

2) Review your own background

Once you learn in general what the position is all about, and what you need to know to do the work, ask yourself which subjects you already know fairly well and which need improvement. You may wonder whether to concentrate on improving your strong areas or on building some background in your fields of weakness. When the announcement has specified "some knowledge" or "considerable knowledge," or has used adjectives like "beginning principles of…" or "advanced … methods," you can get a clue as to the number and difficulty of questions to be asked in any given field. More questions, and hence broader coverage, would be included for those subjects which are more important in the work. Now weigh your strengths and weaknesses against the job requirements and prepare accordingly.

3) Determine the level of the position

Another way to tell how intensively you should prepare is to understand the level of the job for which you are applying. Is it the entering level? In other words, is this the position in which beginners in a field of work are hired? Or is it an intermediate or advanced level? Sometimes this is indicated by such words as "Junior" or "Senior" in the class title. Other jurisdictions use Roman numerals to designate the level – Clerk I, Clerk II, for example. The word "Supervisor" sometimes appears in the title. If the level is not indicated by the title, check the description of duties. Will you be working under very close supervision, or will you have responsibility for independent decisions in this work?

4) Choose appropriate study materials

Now that you know the subjects to be examined and the relative amount of each subject to be covered, you can choose suitable study materials. For beginning level jobs, or even advanced ones, if you have a pronounced weakness in some aspect of your training, read a modern, standard textbook in that field. Be sure it is up to date and has general coverage. Such books are normally available at your library, and the librarian will be glad to help you locate one. For entry-level positions, questions of appropriate difficulty are chosen – neither highly advanced questions, nor those too simple. Such questions require careful thought but not advanced training.

If the position for which you are applying is technical or advanced, you will read more advanced, specialized material. If you are already familiar with the basic principles of your field, elementary textbooks would waste your time. Concentrate on advanced textbooks and technical periodicals. Think through the concepts and review difficult problems in your field.

These are all general sources. You can get more ideas on your own initiative, following these leads. For example, training manuals and publications of the government agency which employs workers in your field can be useful, particularly for technical and professional positions. A letter or visit to the government department involved may result in more specific study suggestions, and certainly will provide you with a more definite idea of the exact nature of the position you are seeking.

III. KINDS OF TESTS

Tests are used for purposes other than measuring knowledge and ability to perform specified duties. For some positions, it is equally important to test ability to make adjustments to new situations or to profit from training. In others, basic mental abilities not dependent on information are essential. Questions which test these things may not appear as pertinent to the duties of the position as those which test for knowledge and information. Yet they are often highly important parts of a fair examination. For very general questions, it is almost impossible to help you direct your study efforts. What we can do is to point out some of the more common of these general abilities needed in public service positions and describe some typical questions.

1) General information

Broad, general information has been found useful for predicting job success in some kinds of work. This is tested in a variety of ways, from vocabulary lists to questions about current events. Basic background in some field of work, such as sociology or economics, may be sampled in a group of questions. Often these are principles which have become familiar to most persons through exposure rather than through formal training. It is difficult to advise you how to study for these questions; being alert to the world around you is our best suggestion.

2) Verbal ability

An example of an ability needed in many positions is verbal or language ability. Verbal ability is, in brief, the ability to use and understand words. Vocabulary and grammar tests are typical measures of this ability. Reading comprehension or paragraph interpretation questions are common in many kinds of civil service tests. You are given a paragraph of written material and asked to find its central meaning.

3) Numerical ability

Number skills can be tested by the familiar arithmetic problem, by checking paired lists of numbers to see which are alike and which are different, or by interpreting charts and graphs. In the latter test, a graph may be printed in the test booklet which you are asked to use as the basis for answering questions.

4) Observation

A popular test for law-enforcement positions is the observation test. A picture is shown to you for several minutes, then taken away. Questions about the picture test your ability to observe both details and larger elements.

5) Following directions

In many positions in the public service, the employee must be able to carry out written instructions dependably and accurately. You may be given a chart with several columns, each column listing a variety of information. The questions require you to carry out directions involving the information given in the chart.

6) Skills and aptitudes

Performance tests effectively measure some manual skills and aptitudes. When the skill is one in which you are trained, such as typing or shorthand, you can practice. These tests are often very much like those given in business school or high school courses. For many of the other skills and aptitudes, however, no short-time preparation can be made. Skills and abilities natural to you or that you have developed throughout your lifetime are being tested.

Many of the general questions just described provide all the data needed to answer the questions and ask you to use your reasoning ability to find the answers. Your best preparation for these tests, as well as for tests of facts and ideas, is to be at your physical and mental best. You, no doubt, have your own methods of getting into an exam-taking mood and keeping "in shape." The next section lists some ideas on this subject.

IV. KINDS OF QUESTIONS

Only rarely is the "essay" question, which you answer in narrative form, used in civil service tests. Civil service tests are usually of the short-answer type. Full instructions for answering these questions will be given to you at the examination. But in case this is your first experience with short-answer questions and separate answer sheets, here is what you need to know:

1) Multiple-choice Questions

Most popular of the short-answer questions is the "multiple choice" or "best answer" question. It can be used, for example, to test for factual knowledge, ability to solve problems or judgment in meeting situations found at work.

A multiple-choice question is normally one of three types—
- It can begin with an incomplete statement followed by several possible endings. You are to find the one ending which *best* completes the statement, although some of the others may not be entirely wrong.
- It can also be a complete statement in the form of a question which is answered by choosing one of the statements listed.

- It can be in the form of a problem – again you select the best answer.

Here is an example of a multiple-choice question with a discussion which should give you some clues as to the method for choosing the right answer:

When an employee has a complaint about his assignment, the action which will *best* help him overcome his difficulty is to
- A. discuss his difficulty with his coworkers
- B. take the problem to the head of the organization
- C. take the problem to the person who gave him the assignment
- D. say nothing to anyone about his complaint

In answering this question, you should study each of the choices to find which is best. Consider choice "A" – Certainly an employee may discuss his complaint with fellow employees, but no change or improvement can result, and the complaint remains unresolved. Choice "B" is a poor choice since the head of the organization probably does not know what assignment you have been given, and taking your problem to him is known as "going over the head" of the supervisor. The supervisor, or person who made the assignment, is the person who can clarify it or correct any injustice. Choice "C" is, therefore, correct. To say nothing, as in choice "D," is unwise. Supervisors have and interest in knowing the problems employees are facing, and the employee is seeking a solution to his problem.

2) True/False Questions

The "true/false" or "right/wrong" form of question is sometimes used. Here a complete statement is given. Your job is to decide whether the statement is right or wrong.

SAMPLE: A roaming cell-phone call to a nearby city costs less than a non-roaming call to a distant city.

This statement is wrong, or false, since roaming calls are more expensive.

This is not a complete list of all possible question forms, although most of the others are variations of these common types. You will always get complete directions for answering questions. Be sure you understand *how* to mark your answers – ask questions until you do.

V. RECORDING YOUR ANSWERS

Computer terminals are used more and more today for many different kinds of exams.

For an examination with very few applicants, you may be told to record your answers in the test booklet itself. Separate answer sheets are much more common. If this separate answer sheet is to be scored by machine – and this is often the case – it is highly important that you mark your answers correctly in order to get credit.

An electronic scoring machine is often used in civil service offices because of the speed with which papers can be scored. Machine-scored answer sheets must be marked with a pencil, which will be given to you. This pencil has a high graphite content which responds to the electronic scoring machine. As a matter of fact, stray dots may register as answers, so do not let your pencil rest on the answer sheet while you are pondering the correct answer. Also, if your pencil lead breaks or is otherwise defective, ask for another.

Since the answer sheet will be dropped in a slot in the scoring machine, be careful not to bend the corners or get the paper crumpled.

The answer sheet normally has five vertical columns of numbers, with 30 numbers to a column. These numbers correspond to the question numbers in your test booklet. After each number, going across the page are four or five pairs of dotted lines. These short dotted lines have small letters or numbers above them. The first two pairs may also have a "T" or "F" above the letters. This indicates that the first two pairs only are to be used if the questions are of the true-false type. If the questions are multiple choice, disregard the "T" and "F" and pay attention only to the small letters or numbers.

Answer your questions in the manner of the sample that follows:

32. The largest city in the United States is
   A. Washington, D.C.
   B. New York City
   C. Chicago
   D. Detroit
   E. San Francisco

1) Choose the answer you think is best. (New York City is the largest, so "B" is correct.)
2) Find the row of dotted lines numbered the same as the question you are answering. (Find row number 32)
3) Find the pair of dotted lines corresponding to the answer. (Find the pair of lines under the mark "B.")
4) Make a solid black mark between the dotted lines.

VI. BEFORE THE TEST

Common sense will help you find procedures to follow to get ready for an examination. Too many of us, however, overlook these sensible measures. Indeed, nervousness and fatigue have been found to be the most serious reasons why applicants fail to do their best on civil service tests. Here is a list of reminders:

- Begin your preparation early – Don't wait until the last minute to go scurrying around for books and materials or to find out what the position is all about.
- Prepare continuously – An hour a night for a week is better than an all-night cram session. This has been definitely established. What is more, a night a week for a month will return better dividends than crowding your study into a shorter period of time.
- Locate the place of the exam – You have been sent a notice telling you when and where to report for the examination. If the location is in a different town or otherwise unfamiliar to you, it would be well to inquire the best route and learn something about the building.
- Relax the night before the test – Allow your mind to rest. Do not study at all that night. Plan some mild recreation or diversion; then go to bed early and get a good night's sleep.
- Get up early enough to make a leisurely trip to the place for the test – This way unforeseen events, traffic snarls, unfamiliar buildings, etc. will not upset you.
- Dress comfortably – A written test is not a fashion show. You will be known by number and not by name, so wear something comfortable.

- Leave excess paraphernalia at home – Shopping bags and odd bundles will get in your way. You need bring only the items mentioned in the official notice you received; usually everything you need is provided. Do not bring reference books to the exam. They will only confuse those last minutes and be taken away from you when in the test room.
- Arrive somewhat ahead of time – If because of transportation schedules you must get there very early, bring a newspaper or magazine to take your mind off yourself while waiting.
- Locate the examination room – When you have found the proper room, you will be directed to the seat or part of the room where you will sit. Sometimes you are given a sheet of instructions to read while you are waiting. Do not fill out any forms until you are told to do so; just read them and be prepared.
- Relax and prepare to listen to the instructions
- If you have any physical problem that may keep you from doing your best, be sure to tell the test administrator. If you are sick or in poor health, you really cannot do your best on the exam. You can come back and take the test some other time.

VII. AT THE TEST

The day of the test is here and you have the test booklet in your hand. The temptation to get going is very strong. Caution! There is more to success than knowing the right answers. You must know how to identify your papers and understand variations in the type of short-answer question used in this particular examination. Follow these suggestions for maximum results from your efforts:

1) Cooperate with the monitor

The test administrator has a duty to create a situation in which you can be as much at ease as possible. He will give instructions, tell you when to begin, check to see that you are marking your answer sheet correctly, and so on. He is not there to guard you, although he will see that your competitors do not take unfair advantage. He wants to help you do your best.

2) Listen to all instructions

Don't jump the gun! Wait until you understand all directions. In most civil service tests you get more time than you need to answer the questions. So don't be in a hurry. Read each word of instructions until you clearly understand the meaning. Study the examples, listen to all announcements and follow directions. Ask questions if you do not understand what to do.

3) Identify your papers

Civil service exams are usually identified by number only. You will be assigned a number; you must not put your name on your test papers. Be sure to copy your number correctly. Since more than one exam may be given, copy your exact examination title.

4) Plan your time

Unless you are told that a test is a "speed" or "rate of work" test, speed itself is usually not important. Time enough to answer all the questions will be provided, but this does not mean that you have all day. An overall time limit has been set. Divide the total time (in minutes) by the number of questions to determine the approximate time you have for each question.

5) Do not linger over difficult questions

If you come across a difficult question, mark it with a paper clip (useful to have along) and come back to it when you have been through the booklet. One caution if you do this – be sure to skip a number on your answer sheet as well. Check often to be sure that you have not lost your place and that you are marking in the row numbered the same as the question you are answering.

6) Read the questions

Be sure you know what the question asks! Many capable people are unsuccessful because they failed to *read* the questions correctly.

7) Answer all questions

Unless you have been instructed that a penalty will be deducted for incorrect answers, it is better to guess than to omit a question.

8) Speed tests

It is often better NOT to guess on speed tests. It has been found that on timed tests people are tempted to spend the last few seconds before time is called in marking answers at random – without even reading them – in the hope of picking up a few extra points. To discourage this practice, the instructions may warn you that your score will be "corrected" for guessing. That is, a penalty will be applied. The incorrect answers will be deducted from the correct ones, or some other penalty formula will be used.

9) Review your answers

If you finish before time is called, go back to the questions you guessed or omitted to give them further thought. Review other answers if you have time.

10) Return your test materials

If you are ready to leave before others have finished or time is called, take ALL your materials to the monitor and leave quietly. Never take any test material with you. The monitor can discover whose papers are not complete, and taking a test booklet may be grounds for disqualification.

VIII. EXAMINATION TECHNIQUES

1) Read the general instructions carefully. These are usually printed on the first page of the exam booklet. As a rule, these instructions refer to the timing of the examination; the fact that you should not start work until the signal and must stop work at a signal, etc. If there are any *special* instructions, such as a choice of questions to be answered, make sure that you note this instruction carefully.

2) When you are ready to start work on the examination, that is as soon as the signal has been given, read the instructions to each question booklet, underline any key words or phrases, such as *least, best, outline, describe* and the like. In this way you will tend to answer as requested rather than discover on reviewing your paper that you *listed without describing*, that you selected the *worst* choice rather than the *best* choice, etc.

3) If the examination is of the objective or multiple-choice type – that is, each question will also give a series of possible answers: A, B, C or D, and you are called upon to select the best answer and write the letter next to that answer on your answer paper – it is advisable to start answering each question in turn. There may be anywhere from 50 to 100 such questions in the three or four hours allotted and you can see how much time would be taken if you read through all the questions before beginning to answer any. Furthermore, if you come across a question or group of questions which you know would be difficult to answer, it would undoubtedly affect your handling of all the other questions.

4) If the examination is of the essay type and contains but a few questions, it is a moot point as to whether you should read all the questions before starting to answer any one. Of course, if you are given a choice – say five out of seven and the like – then it is essential to read all the questions so you can eliminate the two that are most difficult. If, however, you are asked to answer all the questions, there may be danger in trying to answer the easiest one first because you may find that you will spend too much time on it. The best technique is to answer the first question, then proceed to the second, etc.

5) Time your answers. Before the exam begins, write down the time it started, then add the time allowed for the examination and write down the time it must be completed, then divide the time available somewhat as follows:
    - If 3-1/2 hours are allowed, that would be 210 minutes. If you have 80 objective-type questions, that would be an average of 2-1/2 minutes per question. Allow yourself no more than 2 minutes per question, or a total of 160 minutes, which will permit about 50 minutes to review.
    - If for the time allotment of 210 minutes there are 7 essay questions to answer, that would average about 30 minutes a question. Give yourself only 25 minutes per question so that you have about 35 minutes to review.

6) The most important instruction is to *read each question* and make sure you know what is wanted. The second most important instruction is to *time yourself properly* so that you answer every question. The third most important instruction is to *answer every question*. Guess if you have to but include something for each question. Remember that you will receive no credit for a blank and will probably receive some credit if you write something in answer to an essay question. If you guess a letter – say "B" for a multiple-choice question – you may have guessed right. If you leave a blank as an answer to a multiple-choice question, the examiners may respect your feelings but it will not add a point to your score. Some exams may penalize you for wrong answers, so in such cases *only*, you may not want to guess unless you have some basis for your answer.

7) Suggestions
    a. Objective-type questions
        1. Examine the question booklet for proper sequence of pages and questions
        2. Read all instructions carefully
        3. Skip any question which seems too difficult; return to it after all other questions have been answered
        4. Apportion your time properly; do not spend too much time on any single question or group of questions

5. Note and underline key words – *all, most, fewest, least, best, worst, same, opposite,* etc.
6. Pay particular attention to negatives
7. Note unusual option, e.g., unduly long, short, complex, different or similar in content to the body of the question
8. Observe the use of "hedging" words – *probably, may, most likely,* etc.
9. Make sure that your answer is put next to the same number as the question
10. Do not second-guess unless you have good reason to believe the second answer is definitely more correct
11. Cross out original answer if you decide another answer is more accurate; do not erase until you are ready to hand your paper in
12. Answer all questions; guess unless instructed otherwise
13. Leave time for review

   b. Essay questions
   1. Read each question carefully
   2. Determine exactly what is wanted. Underline key words or phrases.
   3. Decide on outline or paragraph answer
   4. Include many different points and elements unless asked to develop any one or two points or elements
   5. Show impartiality by giving pros and cons unless directed to select one side only
   6. Make and write down any assumptions you find necessary to answer the questions
   7. Watch your English, grammar, punctuation and choice of words
   8. Time your answers; don't crowd material

8) Answering the essay question

Most essay questions can be answered by framing the specific response around several key words or ideas. Here are a few such key words or ideas:

M's: manpower, materials, methods, money, management
P's: purpose, program, policy, plan, procedure, practice, problems, pitfalls, personnel, public relations

   a. Six basic steps in handling problems:
   1. Preliminary plan and background development
   2. Collect information, data and facts
   3. Analyze and interpret information, data and facts
   4. Analyze and develop solutions as well as make recommendations
   5. Prepare report and sell recommendations
   6. Install recommendations and follow up effectiveness

   b. Pitfalls to avoid
   1. *Taking things for granted* – A statement of the situation does not necessarily imply that each of the elements is necessarily true; for example, a complaint may be invalid and biased so that all that can be taken for granted is that a complaint has been registered

2. *Considering only one side of a situation* – Wherever possible, indicate several alternatives and then point out the reasons you selected the best one
3. *Failing to indicate follow up* – Whenever your answer indicates action on your part, make certain that you will take proper follow-up action to see how successful your recommendations, procedures or actions turn out to be
4. *Taking too long in answering any single question* – Remember to time your answers properly

IX. AFTER THE TEST

Scoring procedures differ in detail among civil service jurisdictions although the general principles are the same. Whether the papers are hand-scored or graded by machine we have described, they are nearly always graded by number. That is, the person who marks the paper knows only the number – never the name – of the applicant. Not until all the papers have been graded will they be matched with names. If other tests, such as training and experience or oral interview ratings have been given, scores will be combined. Different parts of the examination usually have different weights. For example, the written test might count 60 percent of the final grade, and a rating of training and experience 40 percent. In many jurisdictions, veterans will have a certain number of points added to their grades.

After the final grade has been determined, the names are placed in grade order and an eligible list is established. There are various methods for resolving ties between those who get the same final grade – probably the most common is to place first the name of the person whose application was received first. Job offers are made from the eligible list in the order the names appear on it. You will be notified of your grade and your rank as soon as all these computations have been made. This will be done as rapidly as possible.

People who are found to meet the requirements in the announcement are called "eligibles." Their names are put on a list of eligible candidates. An eligible's chances of getting a job depend on how high he stands on this list and how fast agencies are filling jobs from the list.

When a job is to be filled from a list of eligibles, the agency asks for the names of people on the list of eligibles for that job. When the civil service commission receives this request, it sends to the agency the names of the three people highest on this list. Or, if the job to be filled has specialized requirements, the office sends the agency the names of the top three persons who meet these requirements from the general list.

The appointing officer makes a choice from among the three people whose names were sent to him. If the selected person accepts the appointment, the names of the others are put back on the list to be considered for future openings.

That is the rule in hiring from all kinds of eligible lists, whether they are for typist, carpenter, chemist, or something else. For every vacancy, the appointing officer has his choice of any one of the top three eligibles on the list. This explains why the person whose name is on top of the list sometimes does not get an appointment when some of the persons lower on the list do. If the appointing officer chooses the second or third eligible, the No. 1 eligible does not get a job at once, but stays on the list until he is appointed or the list is terminated.

X. HOW TO PASS THE INTERVIEW TEST

The examination for which you applied requires an oral interview test. You have already taken the written test and you are now being called for the interview test – the final part of the formal examination.

You may think that it is not possible to prepare for an interview test and that there are no procedures to follow during an interview. Our purpose is to point out some things you can do in advance that will help you and some good rules to follow and pitfalls to avoid while you are being interviewed.

What is an interview supposed to test?

The written examination is designed to test the technical knowledge and competence of the candidate; the oral is designed to evaluate intangible qualities, not readily measured otherwise, and to establish a list showing the relative fitness of each candidate – as measured against his competitors – for the position sought. Scoring is not on the basis of "right" and "wrong," but on a sliding scale of values ranging from "not passable" to "outstanding." As a matter of fact, it is possible to achieve a relatively low score without a single "incorrect" answer because of evident weakness in the qualities being measured.

Occasionally, an examination may consist entirely of an oral test – either an individual or a group oral. In such cases, information is sought concerning the technical knowledges and abilities of the candidate, since there has been no written examination for this purpose. More commonly, however, an oral test is used to supplement a written examination.

Who conducts interviews?

The composition of oral boards varies among different jurisdictions. In nearly all, a representative of the personnel department serves as chairman. One of the members of the board may be a representative of the department in which the candidate would work. In some cases, "outside experts" are used, and, frequently, a businessman or some other representative of the general public is asked to serve. Labor and management or other special groups may be represented. The aim is to secure the services of experts in the appropriate field.

However the board is composed, it is a good idea (and not at all improper or unethical) to ascertain in advance of the interview who the members are and what groups they represent. When you are introduced to them, you will have some idea of their backgrounds and interests, and at least you will not stutter and stammer over their names.

What should be done before the interview?

While knowledge about the board members is useful and takes some of the surprise element out of the interview, there is other preparation which is more substantive. It *is* possible to prepare for an oral interview – in several ways:

1) Keep a copy of your application and review it carefully before the interview

This may be the only document before the oral board, and the starting point of the interview. Know what education and experience you have listed there, and the sequence and dates of all of it. Sometimes the board will ask you to review the highlights of your experience for them; you should not have to hem and haw doing it.

2) Study the class specification and the examination announcement

Usually, the oral board has one or both of these to guide them. The qualities, characteristics or knowledges required by the position sought are stated in these documents. They offer valuable clues as to the nature of the oral interview. For example, if the job involves supervisory responsibilities, the announcement will usually indicate that knowledge of modern supervisory methods and the qualifications of the candidate as a supervisor will be tested. If so, you can expect such questions, frequently in the form of a hypothetical situation which you are expected to solve. NEVER go into an oral without knowledge of the duties and responsibilities of the job you seek.

3) Think through each qualification required

Try to visualize the kind of questions you would ask if you were a board member. How well could you answer them? Try especially to appraise your own knowledge and background in each area, *measured against the job sought*, and identify any areas in which you are weak. Be critical and realistic – do not flatter yourself.

4) Do some general reading in areas in which you feel you may be weak

For example, if the job involves supervision and your past experience has NOT, some general reading in supervisory methods and practices, particularly in the field of human relations, might be useful. Do NOT study agency procedures or detailed manuals. The oral board will be testing your understanding and capacity, not your memory.

5) Get a good night's sleep and watch your general health and mental attitude

You will want a clear head at the interview. Take care of a cold or any other minor ailment, and of course, no hangovers.

What should be done on the day of the interview?

Now comes the day of the interview itself. Give yourself plenty of time to get there. Plan to arrive somewhat ahead of the scheduled time, particularly if your appointment is in the fore part of the day. If a previous candidate fails to appear, the board might be ready for you a bit early. By early afternoon an oral board is almost invariably behind schedule if there are many candidates, and you may have to wait. Take along a book or magazine to read, or your application to review, but leave any extraneous material in the waiting room when you go in for your interview. In any event, relax and compose yourself.

The matter of dress is important. The board is forming impressions about you – from your experience, your manners, your attitude, and your appearance. Give your personal appearance careful attention. Dress your best, but not your flashiest. Choose conservative, appropriate clothing, and be sure it is immaculate. This is a business interview, and your appearance should indicate that you regard it as such. Besides, being well groomed and properly dressed will help boost your confidence.

Sooner or later, someone will call your name and escort you into the interview room. *This is it.* From here on you are on your own. It is too late for any more preparation. But remember, you asked for this opportunity to prove your fitness, and you are here because your request was granted.

What happens when you go in?

The usual sequence of events will be as follows: The clerk (who is often the board stenographer) will introduce you to the chairman of the oral board, who will introduce you to the other members of the board. Acknowledge the introductions before you sit down. Do not be surprised if you find a microphone facing you or a stenotypist sitting by. Oral interviews are usually recorded in the event of an appeal or other review.

Usually the chairman of the board will open the interview by reviewing the highlights of your education and work experience from your application – primarily for the benefit of the other members of the board, as well as to get the material into the record. Do not interrupt or comment unless there is an error or significant misinterpretation; if that is the case, do not hesitate. But do not quibble about insignificant matters. Also, he will usually ask you some question about your education, experience or your present job – partly to get you to start talking and to establish the interviewing "rapport." He may start the actual questioning, or turn it over to one of the other members. Frequently, each member undertakes the questioning on a particular area, one in which he is perhaps most competent, so you can expect each member to participate in the examination. Because time is limited, you may also expect some rather abrupt switches in the direction the questioning takes, so do not be upset by it. Normally, a board member will not pursue a single line of questioning unless he discovers a particular strength or weakness.

After each member has participated, the chairman will usually ask whether any member has any further questions, then will ask you if you have anything you wish to add. Unless you are expecting this question, it may floor you. Worse, it may start you off on an extended, extemporaneous speech. The board is not usually seeking more information. The question is principally to offer you a last opportunity to present further qualifications or to indicate that you have nothing to add. So, if you feel that a significant qualification or characteristic has been overlooked, it is proper to point it out in a sentence or so. Do not compliment the board on the thoroughness of their examination – they have been sketchy, and you know it. If you wish, merely say, "No thank you, I have nothing further to add." This is a point where you can "talk yourself out" of a good impression or fail to present an important bit of information. Remember, *you close the interview yourself.*

The chairman will then say, "That is all, Mr. _____, thank you." Do not be startled; the interview is over, and quicker than you think. Thank him, gather your belongings and take your leave. Save your sigh of relief for the other side of the door.

How to put your best foot forward

Throughout this entire process, you may feel that the board individually and collectively is trying to pierce your defenses, seek out your hidden weaknesses and embarrass and confuse you. Actually, this is not true. They are obliged to make an appraisal of your qualifications for the job you are seeking, and they want to see you in your best light. Remember, they must interview all candidates and a non-cooperative candidate may become a failure in spite of their best efforts to bring out his qualifications. Here are 15 suggestions that will help you:

1) **Be natural – Keep your attitude confident, not cocky**

If you are not confident that you can do the job, do not expect the board to be. Do not apologize for your weaknesses, try to bring out your strong points. The board is interested in a positive, not negative, presentation. Cockiness will antagonize any board member and make him wonder if you are covering up a weakness by a false show of strength.

2) **Get comfortable, but don't lounge or sprawl**

Sit erectly but not stiffly. A careless posture may lead the board to conclude that you are careless in other things, or at least that you are not impressed by the importance of the occasion. Either conclusion is natural, even if incorrect. Do not fuss with your clothing, a pencil or an ashtray. Your hands may occasionally be useful to emphasize a point; do not let them become a point of distraction.

3) **Do not wisecrack or make small talk**

This is a serious situation, and your attitude should show that you consider it as such. Further, the time of the board is limited – they do not want to waste it, and neither should you.

4) Do not exaggerate your experience or abilities

In the first place, from information in the application or other interviews and sources, the board may know more about you than you think. Secondly, you probably will not get away with it. An experienced board is rather adept at spotting such a situation, so do not take the chance.

5) If you know a board member, do not make a point of it, yet do not hide it

Certainly you are not fooling him, and probably not the other members of the board. Do not try to take advantage of your acquaintanceship – it will probably do you little good.

6) Do not dominate the interview

Let the board do that. They will give you the clues – do not assume that you have to do all the talking. Realize that the board has a number of questions to ask you, and do not try to take up all the interview time by showing off your extensive knowledge of the answer to the first one.

7) Be attentive

You only have 20 minutes or so, and you should keep your attention at its sharpest throughout. When a member is addressing a problem or question to you, give him your undivided attention. Address your reply principally to him, but do not exclude the other board members.

8) Do not interrupt

A board member may be stating a problem for you to analyze. He will ask you a question when the time comes. Let him state the problem, and wait for the question.

9) Make sure you understand the question

Do not try to answer until you are sure what the question is. If it is not clear, restate it in your own words or ask the board member to clarify it for you. However, do not haggle about minor elements.

10) Reply promptly but not hastily

A common entry on oral board rating sheets is "candidate responded readily," or "candidate hesitated in replies." Respond as promptly and quickly as you can, but do not jump to a hasty, ill-considered answer.

11) Do not be peremptory in your answers

A brief answer is proper – but do not fire your answer back. That is a losing game from your point of view. The board member can probably ask questions much faster than you can answer them.

12) Do not try to create the answer you think the board member wants

He is interested in what kind of mind you have and how it works – not in playing games. Furthermore, he can usually spot this practice and will actually grade you down on it.

13) Do not switch sides in your reply merely to agree with a board member

Frequently, a member will take a contrary position merely to draw you out and to see if you are willing and able to defend your point of view. Do not start a debate, yet do not surrender a good position. If a position is worth taking, it is worth defending.

14) Do not be afraid to admit an error in judgment if you are shown to be wrong

The board knows that you are forced to reply without any opportunity for careful consideration. Your answer may be demonstrably wrong. If so, admit it and get on with the interview.

15) Do not dwell at length on your present job

The opening question may relate to your present assignment. Answer the question but do not go into an extended discussion. You are being examined for a *new* job, not your present one. As a matter of fact, try to phrase ALL your answers in terms of the job for which you are being examined.

Basis of Rating

Probably you will forget most of these "do's" and "don'ts" when you walk into the oral interview room. Even remembering them all will not ensure you a passing grade. Perhaps you did not have the qualifications in the first place. But remembering them will help you to put your best foot forward, without treading on the toes of the board members.

Rumor and popular opinion to the contrary notwithstanding, an oral board wants you to make the best appearance possible. They know you are under pressure – but they also want to see how you respond to it as a guide to what your reaction would be under the pressures of the job you seek. They will be influenced by the degree of poise you display, the personal traits you show and the manner in which you respond.

ABOUT THIS BOOK

This book contains tests divided into Examination Sections. Go through each test, answering every question in the margin. We have also attached a sample answer sheet at the back of the book that can be removed and used. At the end of each test look at the answer key and check your answers. On the ones you got wrong, look at the right answer choice and learn. Do not fill in the answers first. Do not memorize the questions and answers, but understand the answer and principles involved. On your test, the questions will likely be different from the samples. Questions are changed and new ones added. If you understand these past questions you should have success with any changes that arise. Tests may consist of several types of questions. We have additional books on each subject should more study be advisable or necessary for you. Finally, the more you study, the better prepared you will be. This book is intended to be the last thing you study before you walk into the examination room. Prior study of relevant texts is also recommended. NLC publishes some of these in our Fundamental Series. Knowledge and good sense are important factors in passing your exam. Good luck also helps. So now study this Passbook, absorb the material contained within and take that knowledge into the examination. Then do your best to pass that exam.

EXAMINATION SECTION

EXAMINATION SECTION
TEST 1

DIRECTIONS: Each question or incomplete statement is followed by several suggested answers or completions. Select the one that BEST answers the question or completes the statement. *PRINT THE LETTER OF THE CORRECT ANSWER IN THE SPACE AT THE RIGHT.*

1. The CHIEF purpose of a manual of *Instruction & Procedures for Money Room Employees* is to 1.____

    A. describe fully the grievance procedures available to money room employees
    B. describe methods of detecting counterfeit bills, coins, and tokens
    C. describe to money room employees the procedures that are to be used in their work
    D. help prepare money room employees to advance themselves to supervisory positions

2. The Transit, Highway, Bridge & Tunnel Authorities are created by the 2.____

    A. State Legislature   B. Public Service Commission
    C. City Council   D. Congress

3. The amount of money received and counted in the money room varies with the season of the year. 3.____
   Of the following, the CHIEF reason why the money counted is not the same in each season is that there is a seasonal change in the number of

    A. cashiers   B. collecting agents
    C. passengers   D. tollroad clerks

4. The assignments of bill cage cashiers in the money room are rotated so that each cashier verifies receipts from different tollroad clerks each day. 4.____
   The MOST important reason for rotating the cashiers' assignments is that

    A. the cashiers will become more familiar with various aspects of money room procedures
    B. each tollroad clerk remits a different amount of money each day
    C. collusion between cashiers and tollroad clerks is discouraged
    D. usually at least one cashier is absent every day

5. The one of the following for which a tollroad clerk would LEAST likely be held responsible is a counterfeit 5.____

    A. dollar bill   B. half-dollar
    C. nickel   D. token

6. Of the following, the MOST important precaution for a city employee to take when cashing his paycheck is to 6.____

    A. cash the check in a different bank each pay period
    B. endorse the check only when he is about to cash it
    C. insist that the check also be endorsed by the person cashing it
    D. ask the person who will cash the check to properly identify himself

7. In training a new cashier in safety procedures to be followed in the money room, it would be LEAST desirable to explain to him that

   A. the best safety device is a careful man
   B. most accidents are caused by carelessness
   C. it is more important to be careful during his training period than after he has completed his training
   D. he should always be alert to detect any possible hazards in the money room

8. The one of the following which is the SAFEST method for a cashier to use in lifting a heavy money bag is to

   A. bend his knees and back
   B. bend his knees and keep his back straight
   C. keep his knees and back straight
   D. keep his knees straight and bend his back

9. Money room procedures require that dimes, quarters, and half-dollars be bagged in amounts of $1000 each.
   The CHIEF justification for this procedure is that it simplifies the

   A. problem of storage of coins
   B. assigning of work to coin cashiers
   C. counting of money for bank deposit
   D. counting of remittances from tollroad clerks

10. One of the regulations in the money room requires that after $1000 in quarters has been counted and placed in a bag, the bag must be weighed.
    Of the following, the MOST important reason for weighing the bag is to

    A. eliminate the necessity for the bank to recount the money
    B. determine if an error has been made in counting the money
    C. insure against overloading the money truck carrying the money to the bank
    D. make certain that there are no counterfeit coins in the bag

Questions 11-17.

DIRECTIONS: Questions 11 through 17 are to be answered on the basis of the following information.

$100 in pennies weighs 68 pounds; $50 in nickels weighs 11 pounds; $1000 in silver of any denomination weighs 54 pounds; and 1000 tokens valued at $1.50 each weigh 3 pounds, 14 ounces.

11. The weight of $77 in pennies is MOST NEARLY _____ pounds.

    A. 52　　　B. 48　　　C. 54　　　D. 60

12. If the tokens in a bag weigh 1 pound, 15 ounces, then the value of these tokens is

    A. $500　　　B. $750　　　C. $50　　　D. $850

13. The contents of a bag containing halves, dimes, and quarters weigh 38 pounds. 13.____
    The amount of money in the bag is MOST NEARLY

    A. $234   B. $380   C. $760   D. $704

14. The weight of the contents of a bag containing $35 in pennies, $41 in nickels, and $730 14.____
    in silver is

    A. less than 60 pounds
    B. between 60 pounds and 70 pounds
    C. between 71 pounds and 80 pounds
    D. more than 80 pounds

15. In a bag containing 1000 coins, half of the coins are nickels and the other half are dimes. 15.____
    The weight of the coins in the bag is MOST NEARLY _____ pounds.

    A. 8   B. 11   C. 5   D. 75

16. A bag contains $25 in pennies, $200 in quarters, $250 in dimes, and an unspecified 16.____
    amount in nickels.
    If the weight of all the coins in the bag is 60 pounds, then the amount of money, in nickels, is

    A. less than $80   B. between $80 and $90
    C. between $91 and $100   D. more than $100

17. A bag contains $780 in nickels, dimes, and quarters. 17.____
    Of the total number of coins in the bag, 10 percent are dimes, 20 percent are nickels,
    and the rest are quarters. If there are 400 dimes in the bag, then the weight of all the
    coins is

    A. less than 25 pounds
    B. between 25 pounds and 35 pounds
    C. between 36 pounds and 45 pounds
    D. more than 45 pounds

18. 27/64 expressed as a percent is 18.____

    A. 40.6250%   B. 42.1875%   C. 43.7500%   D. 45.3133%

19. $40 reduced by 3/8 of itself is 19.____

    A. $25   B. $65   C. $15   D. $55

20. $1,525.62 minus $397.29 is 20.____

    A. $1137.43   B. $1237.33   C. $1128.33   D. $1127.33

21. 12 1/2 minus 6 1/4 is 21.____

    A. 6 1/4   B. 5 3/4   C. 6 1/2   D. 5 1/2

22. 416 machine bolts $3.75 per hundred will cost 22.____

    A. $.156   B. $156.000   C. $1.560   D. $15.600

23. 21.70 divided by 1.75 equals 23.____

    A. 124.0   B. 12.4   C. 1.24   D. 0.124

24. The number 0.03125 reduced to a common fraction is 24.____
    A. 3/64   B. 1/16   C. 1/32   D. 1/13

25. 7/8 divided by 2/7 is 25.____
    A. 1/4   B. 3 1/16   C. 9/15   D. 4 1/16

26. Men's white linen handkerchiefs cost $1.29 for 3. 26.____
    The cost per dozen handkerchiefs is
    A. $7.75   B. $3.87   C. $14.48   D. $5.16

27. 357 is 6% of 27.____
    A. 2142   B. 5950   C. 4140   D. 5900

28. 572 divided by .52 is 28.____
    A. 1100   B. 110   C. 11.10   D. 11.00

29. The number of decimal places in the product of 0.4266 and 0.3333 is 29.____
    A. 8   B. 6   C. 4   D. 2

30. 72 divided by 0.009 is 30.____
    A. 0.125   B. 800   C. 8000   D. 80

31. Add 5 hrs. 13 min., 3 hrs. 49 min., and 14 min. 31.____
    The sum is _____ hrs. _____ min.
    A. 8; 16   B. 9; 16   C. 9; 76   D. 8; 6

32. The cost of 7 3/4 tons of coal at $20.16 per ton is 32.____
    A. $15.12   B. $151.20   C. $141.12   D. $156.24

33. A salesman gets a commission of 6% on his sales. 33.____
    If he wants his commission to amount to $72, he will have to sell merchandise totaling
    A. $142   B. $1200   C. $120   D. $12

34. The sum of 90.79, 79.09, 97.90, and 9.97 is 34.____
    A. 277.75   B. 278.56   C. 276.94   D. 277.93

35. John Doe borrowed $225,000.00 for 5 years at 8 1/2%. 35.____
    The annual interest charge was
    A. $15,750   B. $15,550   C. $19,125   D. $39,375

KEY (CORRECT ANSWERS)

1.	C	16.	B
2.	A	17.	D
3.	C	18.	B
4.	C	19.	A
5.	D	20.	C
6.	B	21.	A
7.	C	22.	D
8.	B	23.	B
9.	C	24.	C
10.	B	25.	B
11.	A	26.	D
12.	B	27.	B
13.	D	28.	A
14.	C	29.	A
15.	A	30.	C

31. B
32. D
33. B
34. A
35. C

TEST 2

DIRECTIONS: Each question or incomplete statement is followed by several suggested answers or completions. Select the one that BEST answers the question or completes the statement. *PRINT THE LETTER OF THE CORRECT ANSWER IN THE SPACE AT THE RIGHT.*

1. Which number is one more than 4000?
   A. 3099   B. 3900   C. 4001   D. 3999

2. What does MCCXII mean?
   A. 712   B. 512   C. 802   D. 1212

3. What is fifty-two ten-thousandths written as a decimal?
   A. 52,010,000   B. .052   C. .0052   D. .00052

4. What is .127 expressed as a percent?
   A. 12.7%   B. 1.27%   C. 12 7/100%   D. 12 1/2%

5. What is seventy billion forty million sixty in figures?
   A. 70,400,060,000
   B. 70,040,600,000
   C. 70,040,000,060
   D. 70,040,000,600

6. What is the equivalent decimal of the fraction 7/8%?
   A. .875   B. .675   C. .575   D. .785

7. What is the common fraction equivalent (in its lowest terms) of .58 1/3%?
   A. 5/12   B. 174/300   C. 175/100   D. 7/12

8. The Health Department reported that 8 out of 12 children had the measles this spring. What fraction shows what proportion of the children had measles?
   A. 8/20   B. 2/3   C. 1/8   D. 1/12

9. The State census report showed 10,308,252 people in the State. How should this number be written when rounded to the nearest million?
   A. 11,000,000
   B. 10,309,000
   C. 10,308,000
   D. 10,000,000

10. When 3/4% of the people of Seattle have been vaccinated for smallpox, what fraction has been vaccinated?
    A. 3/400   B. 1/75   C. 3/4   D. 4/300

11. What percent of 33 1/3 is 8 1/3?
    A. 66 2/3%   B. 4%   C. 25%   D. 10%

12. The grades received on a clerical examination were as follows: one received a grade of 90; three received 85; four, 80; two, 75; six, 70; five, 65; two, 60; one, 55; one, 50; one, 45; one, 40; one, 30; and one, 25.
    What was the average grade on the examination to the nearest tenth percent?

    A. 85.0%   B. 77.2%   C. 72.7%   D. 66.4%

    12._____

13. A clerk saved 16 2/3% of his salary.
    If his salary was $1800 a month, how many years and months did he work to save $13,500?

    A. 3 years, 9 months   B. 3 years, 6 months
    C. 4 years   D. 3 years, 3 months

    13._____

14. Folders, each containing the same number of sheets, are filed alphabetically in a 4-drawer cabinet. The inside length of each drawer is 35 inches, and all 4 drawers are packed full. Filed under A are 43 folders occupying 7 inches.
    How many folders are there in the whole cabinet?

    A. 20   B. 215   C. 860   D. 645

    14._____

15. A machine operator is paid at the rate of $22.20 per hour if his hourly average production is 250 written bills. For any day in which his hourly average is below 250, his hourly rate of pay is reduced by one-sixth.
    What would be his pay for a seven-hour day in which he produced 1715 written bills?

    A. $129.50   B. $136.90   C. $151.70   D. $155.40

    15._____

16. A stenographer transcribes her notes at the rate of one line typed in ten seconds.
    At this rate, how long (in minutes and seconds) will it take her to transcribe notes which will require seven pages of typing, 25 lines to the page?
    _____ minutes, _____ seconds.

    A. 29; 10   B. 17; 50   C. 40; 10   D. 20; 30

    16._____

17. During one week, a personnel agency receives 192 applications on Monday, 213 on Tuesday, 218 on Wednesday, 215 on Thursday, 102 on Friday, and 194 on Saturday.
    If the agency has seven branch offices, what is the daily average number of applications received in each office for the entire week?

    A. 29   B. 27   C. 189   D. 47

    17._____

18. Pencils used in an office may be bought at the price of two for 10 cents or, when bought in large quantities, at the price of $13.80 for six dozen.
    What is the saving per dozen when pencils are bought at the lower rate?

    A. $.70   B. $1.00   C. $3.70   D. $7.80

    18._____

19. If retirement deductions from salaries are increased from 3 1/2% to 5%, what is the monthly amount of the increase in the deduction from an $18,000 salary?

    A. $15.30   B. $52.50   C. $78.30   D. $22.50

    19._____

20. A man invested $75,000 in a new business enterprise. The first year, he lost .16 2/3 of his original investment. The next year, he made a profit of 1/8 of his net worth at the beginning of that year.
His net worth at the end of the second year was what part of his original investment?

    A. 6 1/4%   B. 75%   C. 80%   D. 93 3/4%

20.____

21. 0.16 3/4 written as a percent is

    A. 16 3/4%   B. 16.3/4%   C. 0.016 3/4%   D. 0.0016 3/4%

21.____

22. $40 reduced by 3/8 of itself is

    A. $25   B. $65   C. $15   D. $55

22.____

23. $1,296.53 minus $264.87 is

    A. $1,232.76   B. $1,032.76   C. $1,031.66   D. $1,132.53

23.____

24. 12 1/2 minus 6 1/4 is

    A. 5 3/4   B. 6 1/4   C. 6 1/2   D. 5 1/2

24.____

25. A desk is marked $98, 20% 30 days, or $98, 30% 15 days cash.
If it is paid for in cash immediately on delivery, the amount paid is

    A. $66.84   B. $63.70   C. $68.40   D. $68.60

25.____

26. Add 1/4, 7/12, 3/8, 1/2, 5/6.

    A. 2 1/2   B. 2 13/24   C. 2 3/4   D. 2 15/24

26.____

27. A floor is 25 ft. wide by 36 ft. long.
To cover this floor with carpet will require _____ square yards.

    A. 100   B. 300   C. 900   D. 25

27.____

28. A salesman gets a commission of 4% on his sales.
If he wants his commission to amount to $40, he will have to sell merchandise totaling

    A. $160   B. $10   C. $1000   D. $100

28.____

29. Add 5 hours, 13 minutes; 3 hours, 49 minutes; and 14 minutes.
The sum is _____ hours, _____ minutes.

    A. 8; 16   B. 9; 16   C. 9; 76   D. 8; 6

29.____

30. John Doe borrowed $425,000 for 5 years at 9 1/2%.
The annual interest charge was

    A. $25,750   B. $35,750   C. $40,375   D. $42,950

30.____

31. 72 divided by .009 is

    A. .125   B. 800   C. 8000   D. 80

31.____

32. 345 locks at $4.15 per hundred will cost

    A. $.1432   B. $1.4320   C. $14.32   D. $143.20

32.____

33. The number which, when decreased by 1/5 of itself equals 132, is   33.____

   A. 165   B. 198   C. 98   D. 88

34. 285 is 5% of   34.____

   A. 1700   B. 7350   C. 1750   D. 5700

35. A store sold suits for $65 each. The suits cost $50 each. The percentage of increase of selling price over cost is   35.____

   A. 40%   B. 33 1/2%   C. 33 1/3%   D. 30%

KEY (CORRECT ANSWERS)

1. C		16. A	
2. D		17. B	
3. C		18. A	
4. A		19. D	
5. C		20. D	
6. A		21. A	
7. D		22. A	
8. B		23. C	
9. D		24. B	
10. A		25. D	
11. C		26. B	
12. D		27. A	
13. A		28. C	
14. C		29. B	
15. A		30. C	

31. C
32. C
33. A
34. D
35. D

EXAMINATION SECTION
TEST 1

DIRECTIONS: Each question or incomplete statement is followed by several suggested answers or completions. Select the one that BEST answers the question or completes the statement. *PRINT THE LETTER OF THE CORRECT ANSWER IN THE SPACE AT THE RIGHT.*

1. The detection of counterfeiting and the apprehension of counterfeiters Is PRIMARILY the responsibility of the

    A. Federal Bureau of Investigation
    B. United States Secret Service
    C. Federal Reserve Board
    D. National Security Council

2. The term *legal tender* applies to

    A. a check, legally endorsed, and intended for deposit only
    B. money which may lawfully be used in the payment of debts
    C. foreign money whose rate of exchange is set by law
    D. uncoined gold or silver in the form of bullion bars

Questions 3-4.

DIRECTIONS: Questions 3 and 4 are to be answered SOLELY on the basis of the information contained in the following statement:

When a design for a new bank note of the Federal Government has been prepared by the Bureau of Engraving and Printing and has been approved by the Secretary of the Treasury, the engravers begin the work of cutting the design in steel. No one engraver does all the work. Each man is a specialist. One works only on portraits, another on lettering, another on scroll work, and so on. Each engraver, with a steel tool known as a graver, and aided by a powerful magnifying glass, carefully carves his portion of the design into the steel. He knows that one false cut or a slip of his tool, or one miscalculation of width or depth of line, may destroy the merit of his work. A single mistake means that months or weeks of labor will have been in vain. The Bureau is proud of the fact that no counterfeiter ever has duplicated the excellent work of its expert engravers.

3. According to the above statement, each engraver in the Bureau of Engraving and Printing

    A. must be approved by the Secretary of the Treasury before he can begin work on the design for a new bank note
    B. is responsible for engraving a complete design of a new bank note himself
    C. designs new bank notes and submits them for approval to the Secretary of the Treasury
    D. performs only a specific part of the work of engraving a design for a new bank note

4. According to the above statement,

A. an engraver's tools are not available to a counterfeiter
B. mistakes made in engraving a design can be corrected immediately with little delay in the work of the Bureau
C. the skilled work of the engravers has not been successfully reproduced by counterfeiters
D. careful carving and cutting by the engravers is essential to prevent damage to equipment

5. The public lays down the rules governing the type of service that it expects to be given. These rules are expressed partly in laws and partly in public opinion, which at any time may be made into law. Private business and government departments have, and always have had, the task of giving the public what it expects, a task which has lately come to be called public relations. According to the above statement,

   A. government departments have the task of serving the public as it wishes to be served
   B. private firms emphasize public relations more than public agencies do
   C. the rules for giving the public the service it expects are all eventually made into laws
   D. the task of public relations is to inform the public about the work of government departments

6. Certain personal qualities are required of an employee who is to perform a particular assignment efficiently. Since each employee possesses different qualities, experience indicates that it is important to seek and select the employee who possesses the personal qualities required for the particular assignment.
According to the above statement,

   A. the personal qualities of an employee should be changed to fit a particular assignment
   B. personal qualities are more important than experience in the performance of an assignment
   C. an assignment should be changed to fit the personal qualities of the employee assigned to it
   D. the employee selected for an assignment should have the personal qualities needed to perform it

7. A cashier has to make many arithmetic calculations in connection with his work. Skill in arithmetic comes readily with practice; no special talent is needed.
On the basis of the above statement, it is MOST accurate to state that

   A. the most important part of a cashier's job is to make calculations
   B. few cashiers have the special ability needed to handle arithmetic problems easily
   C. without special talent, cashiers cannot learn to do the calculations they are required to do in their work
   D. a cashier can, with practice, learn to handle the computations he is required to make

8. A bonded employee is much less likely to be tempted to steal money than an unbonded one, for he knows that a bonding company will prosecute him for the sake of principle, whereas an employer might not ordinarily take any action against an employee if there is no hope of recovering the stolen money.
   The MOST valid implication of the above statement is that

   A. a bonded employee if often tempted to steal because he knows that his employer is protected against the loss
   B. a bonding company will attempt to find and punish the guilty employee even when the stolen money cannot be recovered
   C. an employer whose bonded employees do not steal is wasting the money spent to bond them
   D. it is wasteful for a bonding company to prosecute an employee when there is no chance of recovering the stolen money

   8.____

9. The BEST of the following attitudes regarding departmental rules and regulations for a cashier to take is that they

   A. are simply a means for justifying disciplinary action taken by a supervisor
   B. are to be interpreted by each employee as he sees fit
   C. must be obeyed even if they seem unreasonable in some cases
   D. should be read and studied but may be ignored whenever an employee feels it is necessary to do so

   9.____

10. It is MOST important for a cashier who is assigned to perform a lengthy monotonous task to

    A. perform this task before doing his other work
    B. ask another cashier to assist him to dispose of the task quickly
    C. perform this task only when his other work has been completed
    D. take measures to prevent mistakes in performing this task

    10.____

11. Although accuracy and speed are both important for a cashier in the performance of his work, accuracy should be considered more important MAINLY because

    A. most supervisors insist on accurate work
    B. much time is lost in correcting errors
    C. a rapid rate of work cannot be maintained for any length of time
    D. speedy workers are usually inaccurate

    11.____

12. Of the following, the CHIEF reason why a cashier should not be late to work in the morning is that

    A. he will probably be penalized for his lateness
    B. the work of his unit may be delayed because of his tardiness
    C. he will set a bad example for the other employees to follow
    D. a poor attendance record may affect his supervisor's evaluation of his work

    12.____

13. A cashier who handles large quantities of currency should know that the term *Silver Certificate* usually referred to

    A. a receipt for silver bars deposited with a bank
    B. a form of paper money that is acceptable only for the payment of non-business debts

    13.____

C. a certificate issued by a refiner of silver metal to show the purity of his product
D. a form of paper money that is backed by silver owned by the United States Government

14. There are 12 consecutively numbered Federal Reserve Districts, each having as its symbol a number and the corresponding letter of the alphabet. The Federal Reserve Bank in each district has the same symbol as that of its district. For example, the Federal Reserve Bank of Boston is in the first Federal Reserve District and has as its symbol the number *1* and the letter *A*. The other districts, in numerical order, are New York, Philadelphia, Cleveland, Richmond, Atlanta, Chicago, St. Louis, Minneapolis, Kansas City, Dallas, and San Francisco.
According to the above statement, the Federal Reserve Bank of Philadelphia is represented by the

A. number *2* and the letter *B*
B. number *2* and the letter *C*
C. number *3* and the letter *B*
D. number *3* and the letter *C*

14.____

15. Of the following, the MOST important reason for a cashier to know the portraits that appear on each denomination of paper currency is that

A. he will be able to count bills merely by looking at the portraits
B. familiarity with portraits may help him to identify a counterfeit bill that has had its denomination changed from a lower to a higher amount
C. a greater knowledge of currency may help increase his promotional opportunities
D. the United States Treasury Department sometimes changes the portraits appearing on various currency denominations

15.____

16. The one of the following which is a characteristic of a genuine bill is that its portrait

A. has a fine screen of regular lines in its background
B. has irregular and broken lines in its background
C. has a very dark blue background
D. merges into the background

16.____

17. Of the following characteristics, the one that is LEAST helpful in deciding whether a bill is counterfeit is that the

A. portrait is dull, smudgy or scratchy
B. serial numbers are unevenly spaced
C. geometric lathework is broken and indistinct
D. ink rubs off when the bill is rubbed on a piece of paper

17.____

18. The color of the Treasury seal and serial number on a United States Note is always

A. blue   B. gray   C. green   D. red

18.____

19. The saw teeth points on the rim of the Treasury seal on a genuine bill are generally

A. blunt and uneven   B. broken off and faded
C. indistinct   D. sharp and evenly spaced

19.____

20. If one-half of a mutilated genuine bill is sent to the Currency Redemption Division of the Treasury Department, the bill will   20._____

 A. be redeemed at one-half of its face value
 B. be redeemed at three-fifths of its face value
 C. be redeemed at its full face value
 D. not be redeemed at all

21. The color of the Treasury seal and serial number on a Federal Reserve Note is always   21._____

 A. blue   B. brown   C. green   D. red

22. The serial number on the face of a bill is printed   22._____

 A. to the right of the portrait and to the lower left of the portrait
 B. to the left of the portrait and to the lower right of the portrait
 C. directly above the portrait and directly below the portrait
 D. in the upper left corner and the lower left corner

23. The color of the check letter on the face of a bill is always   23._____

 A. black   B. blue   C. green   D. red

24. The face plate number on the face of a bill is printed in the   24._____

 A. upper left corner   B. upper right corner
 C. lower left corner   D. lower right corner

25. If three-fifths of a mutilated genuine bill is sent to the Currency Redemption Division of the Treasury Department, the bill will   25._____

 A. be redeemed at one-half of its face value
 B. be redeemed at three-fifths of its face value
 C. be redeemed at its full face value
 D. not be redeemed at all

Questions 26 - 35.

DIRECTIONS: In Column I below are listed the names of ten men and buildings. In Column II are listed seven paper currency denominations and a category *None of the above denominations*.

In questions 26 to 35, for each man or building in Column I, print in the correspondingly numbered space on your answer sheet, the capital letter preceding the denomination in Column II on which the man or building appears. If the man or building appears on none of the listed denominations, print the letter *H* in the correspondingly numbered space on your answer sheet.

COLUMN I		COLUMN II	
26.	Alexander Hamilton	A. $1	26.__
27.	White House	B. $2	27.__
28.	Benjamin Franklin	C. $5	28.__
29.	Mount Vernon	D. $10	29.__
30.	Thomas Jefferson	E. $20	30.__
31.	U.S. Treasury Department	F. $50	31.__
32.	Andrew Jackson	G. $100	32.__
33.	United States Capitol	H. None of the above denominations	33.__
34.	George Washington		34.__
35.	Abraham Lincoln		35.__

KEY (CORRECT ANSWERS)

1.	B	11.	B	21.	C	31.	D
2.	B	12.	B	22.	A	32.	E
3.	D	13.	D	23.	A	33.	F
4.	C	14.	D	24.	D	34.	A
5.	A	15.	B	25.	C	35.	C
6.	D	16.	A	26.	D		
7.	D	17.	D	27.	E		
8.	B	18.	D	28.	G		
9.	C	19.	D	29.	H		
10.	D	20.	A	30.	B		

TEST 2

DIRECTIONS: Each question or incomplete statement is followed by several suggested answers or completions. Select the one that BEST answers the question or completes the statement. *PRINT THE LETTER OF THE CORRECT ANSWER IN THE SPACE AT THE RIGHT.*

1. Of the following, the characteristic which describes a genuine coin MOST accurately is that the coin usually   1.____

   A. can be bent easily at the edges
   B. can be cut easily with a knife
   C. has a bell-like ring when dropped on a hard surface
   D. will not bounce when dropped on a hard surface

2. The corrugations on the outer edge of a genuine coin are usually   2.____

   A. even and regular
   B. indistinct and blackened
   C. the same as on a counterfeit coin
   D. uneven and crooked

3. When comparing counterfeit coins with genuine ones, most counterfeit coins usually feel   3.____

   A. greasy   B. cold   C. sticky   D. damp

4. A cashier who, in the course of his duties, suffers even a minor cut should have it properly cared for so that there will be no chance for infection to set in. Amputations, and even deaths, have resulted from small neglected wounds. According to the above statement, it is MOST accurate to state that   4.____

   A. a minor cut is not usually a cause for concern
   B. minor injuries are usually worse than they seem to be
   C. minor injuries should not be neglected
   D. small wounds are more dangerous than big ones

5. Certain types of money may be photographed only with the permission of the Secretary of the Treasury. His permission is not required to photograph   5.____

   A. bills   B. bonds, bills and coins
   C. coins   D. either coins or bills

6. Sometimes in the performance of his duties, a cashier must act alone, without advice from his superior and without reference to any books or other authority for guidance. According to this statement, a cashier must, in the exercise of his duties, sometimes display   6.____

   A. sincerity   B. caution
   C. initiative   D. courtesy

7. To say that a cashier is METICULOUS in the performance of his duties is to say that he is   7.____

   A. extremely careful   B. highly enthusiastic
   C. unusually fast   D. prone to error

8. The word NEGOTIABLE as used in business transactions means MOST NEARLY 8.____

   A. valueless B. transferable
   C. expensive D. profitable

9. An order which is RESCINDED is 9.____

   A. cancelled B. adopted
   C. clarified D. misunderstood

10. The word REMUNERATION means MOST NEARLY 10.____

    A. responsibility B. compensation
    C. complexity D. promotional opportunity

11. Assume that you are a cashier in an agency. Of the following, the MOST important reason why you should be courteous and tactful in dealing with visitors to your agency is that 11.____

    A. some of the visitors may show their appreciation of your courtesy by writing to your supervisor commending your work
    B. visitors who are treated courteously will probably treat you in the same manner
    C. visitors who are treated discourteously may ask your superior to take disciplinary action against you
    D. it is your responsibility to give the visitors a favorable impression of the agency

12. Assume that, as a cashier, you have been assigned the task of training a new employee in the work of collecting payments from the public.
    Of the following, the MOST effective technique to follow in training this employee is for you to 12.____

    A. encourage him by praising the work he has done correctly, but do not show him the mistakes he has made
    B. insist that he obey your instructions completely even if your instructions may not be clear to him
    C. encourage him to ask questions if he does not understand any of the work
    D. give him a complete understanding of his job by showing him the incorrect, as well as the correct ways of doing his work

13. Subtract the total of 9 quarters, 17 dimes and 12 nickels from the total of 6 half-dollars, 14 quarters, 8 dimes and 6 nickels.
    The *answer* is 13.____

    A. $2.05 B. $3.05 C. $3.15 D. $4.15

14. A certified check is one that 14.____

    A. states the purpose for which it is drawn
    B. has funds set aside to cover it by the bank upon which it is drawn
    C. is written by the bank upon which it is drawn
    D. requires the endorsements of both the payee and the maker before it can be cashed

15. Of the following, the MOST accurate description of a cashier's check is that it   15.____
    A. can be cashed only by the cashier of the Bank upon which it is drawn
    B. is drawn by a bank in payment for the services of one of its cashiers
    C. is drawn payable to the cashier of a bank by a depositor of the bank
    D. is drawn by a bank on its own funds and signed by its cashier

16. If, on a check, the amount payable expressed in words and the amount payable expressed in figures are not the same, then the amount payable is the   16.____
    A. amount in figures
    B. amount in words
    C. average of the two amounts
    D. lesser of the two amounts

Questions 17 - 20.

DIRECTIONS: Column I lists four different endorsements that a man named John Doe uses to endorse checks. Column II lists the names of five types of endorsements. In questions 17 to 20, for each endorsement listed in Column I, select the correct name in Column II by which that endorsement is generally known.

On your answer sheet, next to the number corresponding to each type of endorsement listed in Column I, write the capital letter preceding the name listed in Column II by which that endorsement is generally known.

COLUMN I | COLUMN II

17. John Doe | A. blank | 17.____

18. Without recourse John Doe | B. full | 18.____

19. Pay to the order of Richard Roe John Doe | C. qualified | 19.____

20. Pay to the order of City Bank for deposit only John Doe | D. conditional | 20.____

E. restricted

Questions 21 - 25.

DIRECTIONS: Questions 21 to 25 are based on the following table.

COLLECTIONS BY CASHIERS FOR ONE WEEK

Name of Cashier	Monday	Tuesday	Wednesday	Thursday	Friday
Adams	$7487	$7435	$8864	$9264	$9876
Baker	9687	8643	8198	7415	8714
Taylor	7403	'6035	9722	9683	9512
Moore	6869	8212	9417	8933	9463
Foster	9129	9069	7734	8121	9596

21. Of the following, the day of the week on which the MOST money was collected is   21.____
    A. Tuesday   B. Wednesday
    C. Thursday   D. Friday

22. Of the following, the day of the week on which the LEAST money was collected is   22.____

    A. Monday   B. Tuesday
    C. Wednesday   D. Friday

23. The average amount collected per day by all the cashiers is   23.____

    A. less than $42,000
    B. between $42,000 and $42,500
    C. between $42,501 and $43,000
    D. more than $43,000

24. Foster's total collection for Monday, Tuesday and Friday are greater than Taylor's total collections for the same three days by MOST NEARLY   24.____

    A. 12%   B. 17%   C. 21%   D. 83%

25. The average amount collected per cashier on Wednesday   25.____

    A. was less than the average amount collected per cashier on Monday by $328
    B. was greater than the average amount collected per cashier on Monday by $672
    C. was less than the average amount collected per cashier on Thursday by $104
    D. was greater than the average amount collected per cashier on Thursday by $886

26. A bag contains 800 coins. Of these, 10 per cent are dimes, 30 per cent are nickels, and the rest are quarters.   26.____
    The amount of money in the bag is

    A. less than $150   B. between $150 and $300
    C. between $301 and $450   D. more than $450

27. On March 1, the revenue division of a city department counted $800,000. The money counted on March 2 was 10 per cent less than the money counted on March 1. If the money counted on March 3 was 10 per cent greater than the money counted on March 2, then the money counted on March 3 was   27.____

    A. $802,000   B. $792,000
    C. $720,000   D. $700,000

28. If one cashier can count a certain sum of money in 2 hours, and another cashier can count the same sum in 3 hours, then both cashiers working together can count this sum in   28.____

    A. 50 minutes   B. 1 hour and 10 minutes
    C. 1 hour and 12 minutes   D. 1 hour and 20 minutes

29. If the real estate tax is $4.11 per $100 of assessed valuation, the tax on real estate assessed at $19,500 is MOST NEARLY   29.____

    A. $47   B. $650   C. $800   D. $900

30. The tax collections in a tax office for the week ending January 11th were $468,693.80. If this amount was 20 per cent greater than the tax collections for the week ending January 4th, the tax collections for the week ending January 4th were MOST NEARLY   30.____

    A. $328,090   B. $375,000   C. $390,580   D. $393,705

31. Assume that the real estate tax rate is $4.08 per $100 of assessed valuation. If the tax on a house is $1,040.40, then the assessed valuation of the house is   31._____

    A. $25,500
    B. $24,000
    C. $27,000
    D. $28,500

32. Cashier X receives payments from 6 taxpayers every 15 minutes. Cashier Y receives payments from 15 taxpayers every half-hour. If Cashier X begins work at 9 a.m., and Cashier Y begins work at 9:30 a.m., the time at which the two Cashiers will have received payments from an equal number of taxpayers is   32._____

    A. 11 a.m.   B. 11:30 a.m.   C. 12 noon   D. 12:30 p.m.

33. The real estate tax on a piece of real property in a certain city is $1,082.40. If the assessed valuation of the property is $26,400, then the tax rate per $100 of assessed valuation is   33._____

    A. less than $4.05
    B. between $4.05 and $4.08
    C. between $4.09 and $4.14
    D. more than $4.14

34. If $300 is invested at simple interest so as to yield a return of $18 in 9 months, the amount of money that must be invested at the same rate of interest so as to yield a return of $120 in 6 months is   34._____

    A. $3000   B. $3300   C. $2000   D. $2300

35. Mr. Smith is reconciling his bank balance on November 15th by the use of the following information: 35._____
    Balance as per Bank Statement, October 31st - $15,932.20 Total Checks Outstanding, October 31st - 1,642.29 Total Deposits, November 1st to November 15th - 715.00 Total Checks Drawn, November 1st to November
    15th -   1,329.63
    According to the above information, the balance that Mr. Smith's checkbook should show as of the close of business on November 15th is MOST NEARLY

    A. $18,290
    B. $16,647
    C. $13,675
    D. $12,960

KEY (CORRECT ANSWERS)

1. C	11. D	21. D	31. A
2. A	12. C	22. B	32. B
3. A	13. B	23. C	33. C
4. C	14. B	24. C	34. A
5. C	15. D	25. B	35. C
6. C	16. B	26. A	
7. A	17. A	27. B	
8. B	18. C	28. C	
9. A	19. B	29. C	
10. B	20. E	30. C	

———

EFFECTIVELY INTERACTING WITH AGENCY STAFF AND MEMBERS OF THE PUBLIC

Test material will be presented in a multiple-choice question format.

Test Task: You will be presented with a variety of situations in which you must apply knowledge of how best to interact with other people.

SAMPLE QUESTION:

A person approaches you expressing anger about a recent action by your department.
Which one of the following should be your first response to this person?
- A. Interrupt to say you cannot discuss the situation until he calms down.
- B. Say you are sorry that he has been negatively affected by your department's action.
- C. Listen and express understanding that he has been upset by your department's action.
- D. Give him an explanation of the reasons for your department's action.

The CORRECT answer to this sample question is Choice C.
Solution:

Choice A is not correct. It would be inappropriate to interrupt. In addition, saying that you cannot discuss the situation until the person calms down will likely aggravate the person further.

Choice B is not correct. Apologizing for your department's action implies that the action was improper.

Choice C is the correct answer to this question. By listening and expressing understanding that your department's action has upset the person, you demonstrate that you have heard and understand the person's feelings and point of view.

Choice D is not correct. While an explanation of the reasons for the action may be appropriate at a later time, at this moment the person is angry and would not be receptive to such an explanation.

EXAMINATION SECTION
TEST 1

DIRECTIONS: Each question or incomplete statement is followed by several suggested answers or completions. Select the one that BEST answers the question or completes the statement. *PRINT THE LETTER OF THE CORRECT ANSWER IN THE SPACE AT THE RIGHT.*

1. Public organizations usually share each of the following customer-service problems with private organizations EXCEPT
   A. aversion to risk
   B. staff-heaviness
   C. provision of reverse incentives
   D. control-apportionment functions

   1._____

2. A service representative demonstrates interpersonal skills by
   A. identifying a customer's expectations
   B. learning how to use a new office telephone system
   C. studying a competitor's approach to service
   D. anticipating how a customer will react to certain situations

   2._____

3. Of the following, _____ is NOT generally considered to be a common reason for flaws in an organization's customer focus.
   A. commissioned employee compensation
   B. full problem-solving authority for front-line personnel
   C. inadequate hiring practices
   D. specific, case-oriented policy and procedural statements

   3._____

4. According to MOST research, approximately _____ of dissatisfied customers will actually complain or make their dissatisfaction with a product known to the organization.
   A. 5%   B. 25%   C. 50%   D. 75%

   4._____

5. Which of the following is an example of an expected benefit associated with a product or service?
   A. Before buying a car, a customer believes she will not have to take the car in for repairs every few months.
   B. A customer in a sporting goods store tells a salesperson exactly what kind of trolling motor will meet the requirements of the lakes the customer wanted to fish.
   C. A supermarket shopper buys a loaf of bread, believing that the bread will remain fresh for a few days.
   D. An airline passenger discover that the meals served on board are good.

   5._____

6. During a meeting with a service representative, a customer makes an apparently reasonable request. However, the representative knows that satisfying the customer's request will violate a rule that is part of the organization's policy. Although the representative feels that an exception to the rule should be made in this case, she is not sure whether an exception can or should be made.

   6._____

The BEST course of action for the representative would be to
A. deny the request and apologize, explaining the company policy
B. rely on good judgment and allow the request
C. try to steer the customer toward a similar but clearly permissible request
D. contact a manager or more experienced peer to handle the request

7. While organizing an effective customer service department, it would be LEAST effective to
   A. create procedures for relaying reasons for complaints to other departments
   B. set up a clear chain-of-command for handling specific customer complaints
   C. continually monitor performance of front-line personnel
   D. give front-line people full authority to resolve all customer dissatisfaction

8. Of the following, _____ is an example of *tangible* service.
   A. an interior decorator telling his/her ideas to a potential client
   B. a salesclerk giving a written cost estimate to a potential buyer
   C. an automobile salesman telling a showroom customer about a car's performance
   D. a stockbroker offering investment advice over the telephone

9. As a rule, a customer service representative who handles telephones should always answer a call within no more than _____ ring(s).
   A. 1   B. 3   C. 5   D. 8

10. In order to be as useful as possible to an organization, feedback received from customers should NOT be
    A. portrayed on a line graph or similar device
    B. used to provide a general overview
    C. focused on end-use customers
    D. available upon demand

11. Of all the customers who switch to competing organizations approximately _____ percent do so because of poor service.
    A. 25   B. 40   C. 75   D. 95

12. When customers offer information that is incorrect in their complaints, a service representative should do each of the following EXCEPT
    A. assume that the customer is making an innocent mistake
    B. look for opportunities to educate the customer
    C. calmly state a reasonable argument that will correct the customer's mistake
    D. believe the customer until he/she is able to find proof of his/her error

13. In order to insure that a customer feels comfortable in a face-to-face meeting, a service representative should
    A. avoid discussing controversial issues
    B. use personal terms such as *dear* or *friend*
    C. address the customer by his/her first name
    D. tell a few jokes

14. Customer satisfaction is MOST effectively measured in terms of
    A. cost   B. benefit   C. convenience   D. value

15. Making a sale is NOT considered good service when
    A. there are no alternatives to the subject of the customer's complaint
    B. when the original product or service is outdated
    C. an add-in feature will forestall other problems
    D. the product or service the customer has been using is the wrong product

16. When dealing with an indecisive customer, the service representative should
    A. expand available possibilities
    B. offer a way out of unsatisfying decisions
    C. ask probing questions for understanding
    D. steer the customer toward one particular decision

17. Of the following, _____ would NOT be a source of direct organizational service promises.
    A. advertising materials
    B. published organizational policies
    C. contracts
    D. the customer's past experience with the organization

18. Generally, the only kind of organization that can validly circumvent the requirements of customer service is one that
    A. cannot afford to staff an entire service department
    B. relies solely on the sale of ten or fewer items per year
    C. has little or no competition
    D. serves clients that are separated from consumers

19. When using the problem-solving approach to solve the problem of an upset customer, the service representative should FIRST
    A. express respect for the customer
    B. identify the customer's expectations
    C. outline a solution or alternatives
    D. listen to understand the problem

20. During face-to-face meetings with strangers such as service personnel, most North Americans consider a comfortable proximity to be
    A. 6 inches - 1 foot   B. 8 inches - 1½ feet
    C. 1½ - 2 feet   D. 2-4 feet

21. When answering phone calls, a service representative should ALWAYS do each of the following EXCEPT
    A. state his/her name
    B. give the name of the organization or department
    C. ask probing questions
    D. offer assistance

22. If a customer appears to be emotionally neutral when lodging a complaint, it would be MOST appropriate for a service representative to demonstrate ____ in reaction to the complaint.
    A. urgency   B. empathy   C. nonchalance   D. surprise

23. When soliciting customer feedback, standard practice is to limit the number of questions asked to APPROXIMATELY
    A. 3-5   B. 5-10   C. 10-20   D. 15-40

24. A customer has purchased an item from a company and has been told that the item will be delivered in two weeks. However, a customer service representative later discovers that deliveries are running about three days behind schedule.
    The MOST appropriate course of action for the representative would be to
    A. call the customer immediately, apologize for the delay, and await the customer's response
    B. call the customer a few days before delivery is due and explain that the delay is the fault of the delivery company
    C. immediately sent out a *loaner* of the ordered item to the customer
    D. wait for the customer to note the delay and contact the organization

25. Most research show that _____% of what is communicated between people during face-to-face meetings is conveyed through words alone.
    A. 10   B. 30   C. 50   D. 80

KEY (CORRECT ANSWERS)

1. D
2. D
3. B
4. A
5. B

6. D
7. B
8. B
9. B
10. B

11. B
12. C
13. A
14. D
15. A

16. B
17. D
18. C
19. A
20. C

21. C
22. D
23. B
24. A
25. A

TEST 2

DIRECTIONS: Each question or incomplete statement is followed by several suggested answers or completions. Select the one that BEST answers the question or completes the statement. *PRINT THE LETTER OF THE CORRECT ANSWER IN THE SPACE AT THE RIGHT.*

1. When working cooperatively to identify specific internal service targets, personnel typically encounter each of the following obstacles EXCEPT 1.____
    A. rapidly-changing work environment
    B. philosophical differences about the nature of service
    C. specialized knowledge of certain personnel exceeds that of others
    D. a chain-of-command that isolates the end user

2. Which of the following is an example of an external customer relationship? 2.____
    A. Baggage clerks to travelers
    B. Catering staff to flight attendants
    C. Managers to ticketing agents
    D. Maintenance workers to ground crew

3. When a service representative puts a customer's complaint in writing, results will be produced more quickly than if the representative had merely told someone. 3.____
    Which of the following is NOT generally considered to be a reason for this?
    A. The complaint can be more easily routed to parties capable of solving the problem.
    B. Management will understand the problem more clearly.
    C. The representative can more clearly see the main aspects of the complaint.
    D. The complaint and response will become a part of a public record.

4. A customer service representative creates a client file, which contains notes about what particular clients want, need, and expect. 4.____
    Which of the following basic areas of learning is the representative exercising?
    A. Interpersonal skills   B. Product and service knowledge
    C. Customer knowledge   D. Technical skills

5. A customer complains that a desired product, which is currently on sale, is needed in at least two weeks, but the company is out of stock and the product will not be available for another four weeks. 5.____
    Of the following, the BEST example of a service *recovery* on the part of a representative would be to
    A. apologize for the company's inability to serve the customer while expressing a wish to deal with the customer in the future
    B. attempt to steer the customer's interest toward an unrelated product
    C. offer a comparable model at the same sale price

30

6. Of the following, _____ is NOT generally considered to be a function of closed questioning when dealing with a customer.
   A. understanding requests
   B. getting the customer to agree
   C. clarifying what has been said
   D. summarizing a conversation

7. When dealing with a customer who speaks with a heavy foreign accent, a service representative should NOT
   A. speak loudly
   B. speak slowly
   C. avoid humor or witticism
   D. repeat what has been said

8. If a customer service representative is aware that time will be a factor in the delivery of service to a customer, the representative should FIRST
   A. warn the customer that the organization is under time constraints
   B. suggest that the customer return another time
   C. ask the customer to suggest a service deadline
   D. tell the customer when service can reasonably be expected

9. In relation to a customer service representative's view of an organization, the customer's view of the company tends to be
   A. more negative
   B. more objective
   C. broader in scope
   D. less forgiving

10. When asked to define the factors that determine whether they will do business with an organization, most customers maintain that _____ is the MOST important.
    A. friendly employees
    B. having their needs met
    C. convenience
    D. product pricing

11. While a customer is stating her service requirements, a service representative should do each of the following EXCEPT
    A. ask questions about complex or unclear information
    B. formulate a response to the customer's remarks
    C. repeat critical information
    D. attempt to roughly outline the customer's main points

12. If a customer service representative must deal with other member of a service team in order to resolve a problem, the representative should avoid
    A. conveying every single detail of a problem to others
    B. suggesting deadlines for problem resolution
    C. offering opinions about the source of the problem
    D. explaining the specifics concerning the need for resolution

13. Of the following, the LAST step in the resolution of a service problem should be
    A. the offer of an apology for the problem
    B. asking probing questions to understand and conform the nature of the problem
    C. listening to the customer's description of the problem
    D. determining and implementing a solution to the problem

14. _____ is a poor scheduling strategy for a customer service representative.
    A. Performing the easiest tasks first
    B. Varying work routines
    C. Setting deadlines that will allow some restful work periods
    D. Doing similar jobs at the same time

15. The MOST defensible reason for the avoidance of customer satisfaction guarantees is
    A. buyer remorse
    B. repeated customer contact
    C. high costs
    D. ability of buyers to take advantage of guarantees

16. A customer service representative demonstrates knowledge and courtesy to customers and is able to convey trust, competence, and confidence.
    Of the following service factors, the representative is demonstrating
    A. assurance   B. responsiveness
    C. empathy   D. reliability

17. If a service representative is involved in sales, _____ is NOT one of the primary pieces of information he/she will need to supply the customer.
    A. cost of product or service   B. how the product works
    C. how to repair the product   D. available payment plans

18. A customer appears to be experiencing extreme feelings of anger and frustration when loading a complaint.
    The MOST appropriate reaction for a service representative to demonstrate is
    A. urgency   B. empathy   C. nonchalance   D. surprise

19. Of the following obstacles to customer service, _____ is NOT generally considered to be unique to public organizations.
    A. ambivalence toward clients   B. limited competition
    C. a rule-based mission   D. clients who are not really customers

20. Most customers report that the MOST frustrating aspect of waiting in line for service is
    A. not knowing how long they will have to wait for service
    B. rudeness on the part of the service representatives
    C. being expected to wait for service at all
    D. unfair prioritizing on the part of service representatives

21. Which of the following is an example of an *assumed benefit* associated with a product or service?
    A customer
    A buys a sporty sedan and finds that its tight turning ratio makes it easy to park
    B. visits a fast-food restaurant because she is in a hurry to get dinner over with

C. buys a videotape and believes it will not cause damage to her VCR
D. tells a salesman that he wants to purchase a high-status automobile

22. On an average, for every complaint received by an organization, there are actually about _____ customers who have legitimate problems.
    A. 3
    B. 5
    C. 15
    D. 25

23. Once a customer problem is identified, each of the following should become a part of the service recovery process EXCEPT
    A. apologizing
    B. an offer of compensation
    C. empathetic listening
    D. sympathy

24. As a rule, customers who telephone organizations should not be put on hold for any longer than
    A. 10 seconds
    B. 60 seconds
    C. 5 minutes
    D. 10 minutes

25. The LEAST effective way to make customers feel as if they are a part of a service team would be to ask them for
    A. information about similar products/services they have used
    B. opinions about how to solve problems
    C. personally contact the department that can best help them
    D. opinions about particular products and services

KEY (CORRECT ANSWERS)

1.	B	11.	B
2.	A	12.	C
3.	D	13.	A
4.	C	14.	A
5.	D	15.	B
6.	A	16.	A
7.	A	17.	C
8.	C	18.	B
9.	C	19.	B
10.	B	20.	A

21. C
22. D
23. D
24. B
25. C

CLERICAL ABILITIES TEST

Clerical aptitude involves the ability to perceive pertinent detail in verbal or tabular material, to observe differences in copy, to proofread words and numbers, and to avoid perceptual errors in arithmetic computation.

NATURE OF THE TEST

Four types of clerical aptitude questions are presented in the Clerical Abilities Test. There are 120 questions with a short time limit. The test contains 30 questions on name and number checking, 30 on the arrangement of names in correct alphabetical order, 30 on simple arithmetic, and 30 on inspecting groups of letters and numbers. The questions have been arranged in groups or cycles of five questions of each type. The Clerical Abilities Test is primarily a test of speed in carrying out relatively simple clerical tasks. While accuracy on these tasks is important and will be taken into account in the scoring, experience has shown that many persons are so concerned about accuracy that they do the test more slowly than they should. Competitors should be cautioned that speed as well as accuracy is important to achieve a good score.

HOW THE TEST IS ADMINISTERED

Each competitor should be given a copy of the test booklet with sample questions on the cover page, an answer sheet, and a medium No. 2 pencil. Ten minutes are allowed to study the directions and sample questions and to answer the questions in the proper boxes on the two pages.
The separate answer sheet should be used for the test proper. Fifteen minutes are allowed for the test.

HOW THE TEST IS SCORED

The correct answers should be counted and recorded. The number of incorrect answers must also be counted because one-fourth of the number of incorrect answers is subtracted from the number of right answers. An omission is considered as neither a right nor a wrong answer. The score on this test is the number of right answers minus one-fourth of the number of wrong answers (fractions of one-half or less are dropped). For example, if an applicant had answered 89 questions correctly and 10 questions incorrectly, and had omitted 1 question, his score would be 87.

EXAMINATION SECTION

DIRECTIONS: This test contains four kinds of questions. There are some of each kind on each page in the booklet. The time limit for the test will be announced by the examiner.
Use the special pencil furnished by the examiner in marking your answers on the separate answer sheet. For each question, there are five suggested answers. Decide which answer is correct, find the number of the question on the answer sheet, and make a solid black mark between the dotted lines just below the letter of your answer. If you wish to change your answer, erase the first mark completely, do not merely cross it out.

SAMPLE QUESTIONS

In each line across the page there are three names or numbers that are much alike. Compare the three names or numbers and decide which ones are exactly alike. On the Sample Answer Sheet at the right, mark the answer
   A. if ALL THREE names or numbers are exactly ALIKE
   B. if only the FIRST and SECOND names or numbers are exactly ALIKE
   C. if only the FIRST and THIRD names or numbers are exactly ALIKE
   D. if only the SECOND and THIRD names or numbers are exactly ALIKE
   E. if ALL THREE names or numbers are DIFFERENT

I.	Davis Hazen	David Hozen	David Hazen
II.	Lois Appel	Lois Appel	Lois Apfel
III.	June Allan	Jane Allan	Jane Allan
IV.	10235	10235	10235
V.	32614	32164	32614

It will be to your advantage to learn what A, B, C, D, and E stand for. If you finish the sample questions before you are told to turn to the test, study them.

SAMPLE ANSWER SHEET

	A	B	C	D	E
I					
II					
III					
IV					
V					
VI					
VII					

In the next group of sample questions, there is a name in a box at the left, and four other names in alphabetical order at the right. Find the correct space for the boxed name so that it will be in alphabetical order with the others, and mark the letter of that space as your answer.

VI. | Jones, Jane |

A. →
   Goodyear, G.L.
B. →
   Haddon, Harry
C. →
   Jackson, Mary
D. →
   Jenkins, William
E. →

VII. | Kessler, Neilson |

A. →
   Kessel, Carl
B. →
   Kessinger, D.J.
C. →
   Kessler, Karl
D. →
   Kessner, Lewis
E. →

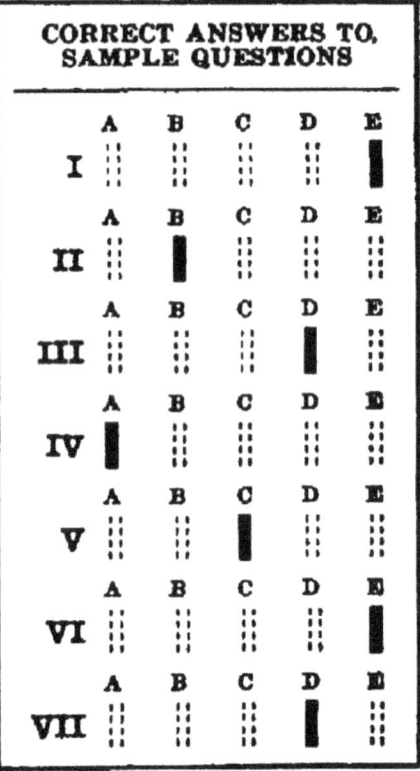

DIRECTIONS: In the following questions, complete the equation and find your answer among the list of suggested answers. Mark the Sample Answer Sheet A, B, C, or D for the answer you obtained; or if your answer is not among these, mark E for that question.

VIII. Add: 22
        +33

  A. 44   B. 45   C. 54   D. 55   E. None of these

IX. Subtract: 24
            - 3

  A. 20   B. 21   C. 27   D. 29   E. None of these

X. Multiply: 25
           x 5

  A. 100   B. 115   C. 125   D. 135   E. None of these

XI. Divide: 6/126̄

    A. 20   B. 22   C. 24   D. 26   E. None of these

DIRECTIONS: There is one set of suggested answers for the next group of sample questions. Do not try to memorize these answers, because there will be a different set on each age in the test.

To find the answer to a question, find which suggested answer contains numbers and letters, all of which appear in the question. If no suggested answer fits, mark E for that question.

XII. 8 N K 9 G T 4 6

XIII. T 9 7 Z 6 L 3 K

XIV. Z 7 G K 3 9 8 N

XV. 3 K 9 4 6 G Z L

XVI. Z N 7 3 8 K T 9

Suggested Answers
A = 7, 9, G, K
B = 8, 9, T, Z
C = 6, 7, K, Z
D = 6, 8, G, T
E = None of the above

After you have marked your answers to all the questions on the Sample Answer Sheets on this page and on the front page of the booklet, check them with the answers in the boxes marked Correct Answers To Sample Questions.

Questions 1-5.

In Questions 1 through 5, compare the three names or numbers, and mark
    A. if ALL THREE names or numbers are exactly ALIKE
    B. if only the FIRST and SECOND names or numbers are exactly ALIKE
    C. if only the FIRST and THIRD names or numbers are exactly ALIKE
    D. if only the SECOND and THIRD names or numbers are exactly ALIKE
    E. if ALL THREE names or numbers are DIFFERENT

1.   5261383   5261383   5261338

2.   8125690   8126690   8125609

3.   W.E. Johnston   W.E. Johnson   W.E. Johnson

4.   Vergil L. Muller   Vergil L. Muller   Vergil L. Muller

5.   Atherton R. Warde   Asheton R. Warde   Atherton P. Warde

Questions 6-10.

In Questions 6 through 10, find the correct place for the name in the box

6. | Hackett, Gerald |

   A. →
      Habert, James
   B. →
      Hachett, J.J.
   C. →
      Hachetts, K. Larson
   D. →
      Hachettson, Leroy
   E. →

7. | Margenroth, Alvin |

   A. →
      Margeroth, Albert
   B. →
      Margestein, Dan
   C. →
      Margestein, David
   D. →
      Margue, Edgar
   E. →

8. | Bobbitt, Olivier E. |

   A. →
      Bobbitt, D. Olivier
   B. →
      Bobbitt, Olivia B
   C. →
      Bobbitt, Olivia H.
   D. →
      Bobbitt, R. Olivia
   E. →

9. | Mosley, Werner |

   A. →
      Mosely, Albert J.
   B. →
      Mosley, Alvin
   C. →
      Mosley, S.M.
   D. →
      Mozley, Vinson N.
   E. →

10. | Youmuns, Frank L. |

A. →
   Youmons, Frank G.
B. →
   Youmons, Frank H.
C. →
   Youmons, Frank K.
D. →
   Youmons, Frank M.
E. →

Questions 11-15.

11. Add: 43
         +32

    A. 55   B. 65   C. 66   D. 75   E. None of these

12. Subtract: 83
              - 4

    A. 73   B. 79   C. 80   D. 89   E. None of these

13. Multiply: 41
              x 7

    A. 281   B. 287   C. 291   D. 297   E. None of these

14. Divide: 6/306

    A. 44   B. 51   C. 52   D. 60   E. None of these

15. Add: 37
         +15

    A. 42   B. 52   C. 53   D. 62   E. None of these

Questions 16-20.

In Questions 16 through 20, find which one of the suggested answers appears in that question.

16. 6 2 5 K 4 P T G

17. L 4 7 2 T 6 V K

18. 3 5 4 L 9 V T G

19. G 4 K 7 L 3 5 Z

SUGGESTED ANSWERS
A = 4, 5, K, T
B = 4, 7, G, K
C = 2, 5, G, L
D = 2, 7, L, T
E = None of the above

20. 4 K 2 9 N 5 T G

Questions 21-25.

In Questions 21 through 25, compare the three names or numbers, and mark
  A. if ALL THREE names or numbers are exactly ALIKE
  B. if only the FIRST and SECOND names or numbers are exactly ALIKE
  C. if only the FIRST and THIRD names or numbers are exactly ALIKE
  D. if only the SECOND and THIRD names or numbers are exactly ALIKE
  E. if ALL THREE names or numbers are DIFFERENT

21.	2395890	2395890	2395890
22.	1926341	1926347	1926314
23.	E. Owens McVey	E. Owen McVey	E. Owen McVay
24.	Emily Neal Rouse	Emily Neal Rowse	Emily Neal Rowse
25.	H. Merritt Audubon	H. Merriott Audubon	H. Merritt Audubon

Questions 26-30.

In Questions 26 through 30, find the correct place for the name in the box.

26. Watters, N.O.
  A. →
     Waters, Charles L.
  B. →
     Waterson, Nina P.
  C. →
     Watson, Nora J.
  D. →
     Wattwood, Paul A.
  E. →

27. Johnston, Edward
  A. →
     Johnston, Edgar R.
  B. →
     Johnston, Edmond
  C. →
     Johnston, Edmund
  D. →
     Johnstone, Edmund A.
  E. →

28. | Rensch, Adeline |

A. →
    Ramsay, Amos
B. →
    Remschel, Augusta
C. →
    Renshaw, Austin
D. →
    Rentzel, Becky
E. →

29. | Schnyder, Maurice |

A. →
    Schneider, Martin
B. →
    Schneider, Mertens
C. →
    Schnyder, Newman
D. →
    Schreibner, Norman
E. →

30. | Freedenburg, C. Erma |

A. →
    Freedenberg, Emerson
B. →
    Freedenberg, Erma
C. →
    Freedenberg, Erma E.
D. →
    Freedinberg, Erma F.
E. →

Questions 31-35.

31. Subtract: 68
              - 47

    A. 10   B. 11   C. 20   D. 22   E. None of these

32. Multiply: 50
               x 8

    A. 400   B. 408   C. 450   D. 458   E. None of these

33. Divide: 9/180

    A. 20   B. 29   C. 30   D. 39   E. None of these

34. Add: 78
             + 63

    A. 131   B. 140   C. 141   D. 151   E. None of these

35. Add: 89
         + 70

    A. 9   B. 18   C. 19   D. 29   E. None of these

Questions 36-40.

In Questions 36 through 40, find which one of the suggested answers appears in that question.

36. 9 G Z 3 L 4 6 N

37. L 5 N K 4 3 9 V

38. 8 2 V P 9 L Z 5

39. V P 9 Z 5 L 8 7

40. 5 T 8 N 2 9 V L

SUGGESTED ANSWERS
A = 4, 9, L, V
B = 4, 5, N, Z
C = 5, 8, L, Z
D = 8, 9, N, V
E = None of the above

Questions 41-45.

In Questions 41 through 45, compare the three names or numbers, and mark
    A. if ALL THREE names or numbers are exactly ALIKE
    B. if only the FIRST and SECOND names or numbers are exactly ALIKE
    C. if only the FIRST and THIRD names or numbers are exactly ALIKE
    D. if only the SECOND and THIRD names or numbers are exactly ALIKE
    E. if ALL THREE names or numbers are DIFFERENT

41.	6219354	621354	6219354
42.	2312793	2312793	2312793
43.	1065407	1065407	1065047
44.	Francis Ransdell	Frances Ramsdell	Francis Ramsdell
45.	Cornelius Detwiler	Cornelius Detwiler	Cornelius Detwiler

Questions 46-50.

In Questions 46 through 50, find the correct place for the name in the box.

46. | DeMattia, Jessica |

A. →
DeLong, Jesse
B. →
DeMatteo, Jessie
C. →
Derby, Jessie S.
D. →
DeShazo, L.M.
E. →

47. | Theriault, Louis |

A. →
Therien, Annette
B. →
Therien, Elaine
C. →
Thibeault, Gerald
D. →
Thiebeault, Pierre
E. →

48. | Gaston, M. Hubert |

A. →
Gaston, Dorothy M.
B. →
Gaston, Henry N.
C. →
Gaston, Isabel
D. →
Gaston, M. Melvin
E. →

49. | SanMiguel, Carlos |

A. →
SanLuis, Juana
B. →
Santilli, Laura
C. →
Stinnett, Nellie
D. →
Stoddard, Victor
E. →

50. | DeLaTour, Hall F. |

A. →
   DeLargy, Harold
B. →
   DeLathouder, Hilda
C. →
   Lathrop, Hillary
D. →
   LaTour, Hulbert E.
E. →

Questions 51-55.

51. Multiply: 62
              x 5

    A. 300   B. 310   C. 315   D. 360   E. None of these

52. Divide: 3/153

    A. 41   B. 43   C. 51   D. 53   E. None of these

53. Add: 47
         +21

    A. 58   B. 59   C. 67   D. 68   E. None of these

54. Subtract: 87
              - 42

    A. 34   B. 35   C. 44   D. 45   E. None of these

55. Multiply: 37
              x 3

    A. 91   B. 101   C. 104   D. 114   E. None of these

Questions 56-60.

For Questions 56 through 60, find which one of the suggested answers appears in that question.

56. N 5 4 7 T K 3 Z

57. 8 5 3 V L 2 Z N

58. 7 2 5 N 9 K L V

59. 9 8 L 2 5 Z K V

60. Z 6 5 V 9 3 P N

SUGGESTED ANSWERS
A = 3, 8, K, N
B = 5, 8, N, V
C = 3, 9, V, Z
D = 5, 9, K, Z
E = None of the above

Questions 61-65.

In Questions 61 through 65, compare the three names or numbers, and mark
- A. if ALL THREE names or numbers are exactly ALIKE
- B. if only the FIRST and SECOND names or numbers are exactly ALIKE
- C. if only the FIRST and THIRD names or numbers are exactly ALIKE
- D. if only the SECOND and THIRD names or numbers are exactly ALIKE
- E. if ALL THREE names or numbers are DIFFERENT

61.	6452054	6452654	6452054
62.	8501268	8501268	8501286
63	Ella Burk Newham	Ella Burk Newnham	Elena Burk Newnham
64.	Jno. K. Ravencroft	Jno. H. Ravencroft	Jno. H. Ravencoft
65.	Martin Wills Pullen	Martin Wills Pulen	Martin Wills Pullen

Questions 66-70.

In Questions 66 through 70, find the correct place for the name in the box.

66. | O'Bannon, M.J. |

- A. →
- O'Beirne, B.B.
- B. →
- Oberlin, E.L.
- C. →
- Oberneir, L.P.
- D. →
- O'Brian, S.F.
- E. →

67. | Entsminger, Jacob |

- A. →
- Ensminger, J.
- B. →
- Entsminger, J.A.
- C. →
- Entsminger, Jack
- D. →
- Entsminger, James
- E. →

68. | Iacone, Pete R. |

A. →
Iacone, Pedro
B. →
Iacone, Pedro M.
C. →
Iacone, Peter F.
D. →
Iascone, Peter W.
E. →

69. | Sheppard, Gladys |

A. →
Shepard, Dwight
B. →
Shepard, F.H.
C. →
Shephard, Louise
D. →
Shepperd, Stella
E. →

70. | Thackton, Melvin T. |

A. →
Thackston, Milton G.
B. →
Thackston, Milton W.
C. →
Thackston, Theodore
D. →
Thackston, Thomas G.
E. →

Questions 71-75.

71. Divide: $7\overline{)357}$

   A. 51   B. 52   C. 53   D. 54   E. None of these

72. Add: 58
         +27

   A. 75   B. 84   C. 85   D. 95   E. None of these

73. Subtract: 86
              - 57

   A. 18   B. 29   C. 38   D. 39   E. None of these

74. Multiply: 68
        x 4

   A. 242   B. 264   C. 272   D. 274   E. None of these

75. Divide: 9/639

   A. 71   B. 73   C. 81   D. 83   E. None of these

Questions 76-80.

For Questions 76 through 80, find which one of the suggested answers appears in that question.

76. 6 Z T N 8 7 4 V

77. V 7 8 6 N 5 P L

78. N 7 P V 8 4 2 L

79. 7 8 G 4 3 V L T

80. 4 8 G 2 T N 6 L

SUGGESTED ANSWERS
A = 2, 7, L, N
B = 2, 8, T, V
C = 6, 8, L, T
D = 6, 7, N, V
E = None of the above

Questions 81-85.

In Questions 81 through 85, compare the three names or numbers, and mark
    A. if ALL THREE names or numbers are exactly ALIKE
    B. if only the FIRST and SECOND names or numbers are exactly ALIKE
    C. if only the FIRST and THIRD names or numbers are exactly ALIKE
    D. if only the SECOND and THIRD names or numbers are exactly ALIKE
    E. if ALL THREE names or numbers are DIFFERENT

81.	3457988	3457986	3457986
82.	4695682	4695862	4695682
83.	Stricklund Kanedy	Stricklund Kanedy	Stricklund Kanedy
84.	Joy Harbor Witner	Joy Harloe Witner	Joy Harloe Witner
85.	R.M.O. Uberroth	R.M.O. Uberroth	R.N.O. Uberroth

Questions 86-90.

In Questions 86 through 90, find the correct place for the name in the box.

86. | Dunlavey, M. Hilary |

A. →
Dunleavy, Hilary G.
B. →
Dunleavy, Hilary K.
C. →
Dunleavy, Hilary S.
D. →
Dunleavy, Hilery W.
E. →

87. | Yarbrough, Maria |

A. →
Yabroudy, Margy
B. →
Yarboro, Marie
C. →
Yarborough, Marina
D. →
Yarborough, Mary
E. →

88. | Prouty, Martha |

A. →
Proutey, Margaret
B. →
Proutey, Maude
C. →
Prouty, Myra
D. →
Prouty, Naomi
E. →

89. | Pawlowicz, Ruth M. |

A. →
Pawalek, Edward
B. →
Pawelek, Flora G.
C. →
Pawlowski, Joan M.
D. →
Pawtowski, Wanda
E. →

90. | Vanstory, George |

A. →
   Vanover, Eva
B. →
   VanSwinderen, Floyd
C. →
   VanSyckle, Harry
D. →
   Vanture, Laurence
E. →

Questions 91-95

91. Add: 28
         +35

   A. 53   B. 62   C. 64   D. 73   E. None of these

92. Subtract: 78
             -69

   A. 7   B. 8   C. 18   D. 19   E. None of these

93. Multiply: 86
             x 6

   A. 492   B. 506   C. 516   D. 526   E. None of these

94. Divide: 8/648

   A. 71   B. 76   C. 81   D. 89   E. None of these

95. Add: 97
         +34

   A. 131   B. 132   C. 140   D. 141   E. None of these

Questions 96-100.

For Questions 96 through 100, find which one of the suggested answers appears in that question.

96. V 5 7 Z N 9 4 T

97. 4 6 P T 2 N K 9

98. 6 4 N 2 P 8 Z K

99. 7 P 5 2 4 N K T

100. K T 8 5 4 N 2 P

SUGGESTED ANSWERS
A = 2, 5, N, Z
B = 4, 5, N, P
C = 2, 9, P, T
D = 4, 9, T, Z
E = None of the above

Questions 101-105.

In Questions 101 through 105, compare the three names or numbers, and mark
- A. if ALL THREE names or numbers are exactly ALIKE
- B. if only the FIRST and SECOND names or numbers are exactly ALIKE
- C. if only the FIRST and THIRD names or numbers are exactly ALIKE
- D. if only the SECOND and THIRD names or numbers are exactly ALIKE
- E. if ALL THREE names or numbers are DIFFERENT

101.	1592514	1592574	1592574
102.	2010202	2010202	2010220
103.	6177396	6177936	6177396
104.	Drusilla S. Ridgeley	Drusilla S. Ridgeley	Drusilla S. Ridgeley
105.	Andrei I. Toumantzev	Andrei I. Tourmantzev	Andrei I. Toumantzov

Questions 106-110.

In Questions 106 through 110, find the correct place for the name in the box.

106. Fitzsimmons, Hugh

A. →
Fitts, Harold
B. →
Fitzgerald, June
C. →
FitzGibbon, Junius
D. →
FitzSimons, Martin
E. →

107. D'Amato, Vincent

A. →
Daly, Steven
B. →
D'Amboise, S. Vincent
C. →
Daniel, Vail
D. →
DeAlba, Valentina
E. →

108. | Schaeffer, Roger D. |

    A. →
       Schaffert, Evelyn M.
    B. →
       Schaffner, Margaret M.
    C. →
       Schafhirt, Milton G.
    D. →
       Shafer, Richard E.
    E. →

109. | White-Lewis, Cecil |

    A. →
       Whitelaw, Cordelia
    B. →
       White-Leigh, Nancy
    C. →
       Whitely, Rodney
    D. →
       Whitlock, Warren
    E. →

110. | VanDerHeggen, Don |

    A. →
       VanDemark, Doris
    B. →
       Vandenberg, H.E.
    C. →
       VanDercook, Marie
    D. →
       vanderLinden, Robert
    E. →

Questions 111-115.

111. Add: 75
       +49

    A. 124   B. 125   C. 134   D. 225   E. None of these

112. Subtract: 69
           - 45

    A. 14   B. 23   C. 24   D. 26   E. None of these

113. Multiply: 36
          x 8

    A. 246   B. 262   C. 288   D. 368   E. None of these

114. Divide: 8/͞3͞2͞8͞

    A. 31   B. 41   C. 42   D. 48   E. None of these

115. Multiply: 58
                x 9

    A. 472   B. 513   C. 521   D. 522   E. None of these

Questions 116-120.

For Questions 116 through 120, find which one of the suggested answers appears in that question.

116. Z 3 N P G 5 4 2

117. 6 N 2 8 G 4 P T

118. 6 N 4 T V G 8 2

119. T 3 P 4 N 8 G 2

120. 6 7 K G N 2 L 5

SUGGESTED ANSWERS:
A = 2, 3, G, N
B = 2, 6, N, T
C = 3, 4, G, K
D = 4, 6, K, T
E = None of the above

KEY (CORRECT ANSWERS)

1. B	21. A	41. A	61. C	81. D	101. D
2. E	22. E	42. A	62. B	82. C	102. B
3. D	23. E	43. B	63. E	83. A	103. C
4. A	24. D	44. E	64. E	84. D	104. A
5. E	25. C	45. A	65. C	85. B	105. E
6. E	26. D	46. C	66. A	86. A	106. D
7. A	27. D	47. A	667. D	87. E	107. B
8. D	28. C	48. D	68. C	88. C	108. A
9. B	29. C	49. B	69. D	89. C	109. C
10. E	30. D	50. C	70. E	90. B	110. D
11. D	31. E	51. B	71. A	91. E	111. A
12. B	32. A	52. C	72. C	92. E	112. C
13. B	33. A	53. D	73. B	93. C	113. C
14. B	34. C	54. D	74. C	94. C	114. B
15. B	35. C	55. E	75. A	95. A	115. D
16. A	36. E	56. E	76. D	96. D	116. A
17. D	37. A	57. B	77. D	97. C	117. B
18. E	38. C	58. E	78. A	98. E	118. B
19. B	39. C	59. D	79. E	99. B	119. A
20. A	40. D	60. C	80. C	100. B	120. E

CLERICAL ABILITIES
EXAMINATION SECTION
TEST 1

DIRECTIONS: Each question or incomplete statement is followed by several suggested answers or completions. Select the one that BEST answers the question or completes the statement. *PRINT THE LETTER OF THE CORRECT ANSWER IN THE SPACE AT THE RIGHT.*

Questions 1-4.

DIRECTIONS: Questions 1 through 4 are to be answered on the basis of the information given below.

The most commonly used filing system and the one that is easiest to learn is alphabetical filing. This involves putting records in an A to Z order, according to the letters of the alphabet. The name of a person is filed by using the following order: first, the surname or last name; second, the first name; third, the middle name or middle initial. For example, *Henry C. Young* is filed under *Y* and thereafter under *Young, Henry C.* The name of a company is filed in the same way. For example, *Long Cabinet Co.* is filed under *L* while *John T. Long Cabinet Co.* is filed under *L* and thereafter under *Long, John T. Cabinet Co.*

1. The one of the following which lists the names of persons in the CORRECT alphabetical order is:
   A. Mary Carrie, Helen Carrol, James Carson, John Carter
   B. James Carson, Mary Carrie, John Carter, Helen Carrol
   C. Helen Carrol, James Carson, John Carter, Mary Carrie
   D. John Carter, Helen Carrol, Mary Carrie, James Carson

   1.____

2. The one of the following which lists the names of persons in the CORRECT alphabetical order is:
   A. Jones, John C.; Jones, John A.; Jones, John P.; Jones, John K.
   B. Jones, John P.; Jones, John K.; Jones, John C.; Jones, John A.
   C. Jones, John A.; Jones, John C.; Jones, John K.; Jones, John P.
   D. Jones, John K.; Jones, John C.; Jones, John A.; Jones, John P.

   2.____

3. The one of the following which lists the names of the companies in the CORRECT alphabetical order is:
   A. Blane Co., Blake Co., Block Co., Blear Co.
   B. Blake Co., Blane Co., Blear Co., Block Co.
   C. Block Co., Blear Co., Blane Co., Blake Co.
   D. Blear Co., Blake Co., Blane Co., Block Co.

   3.____

4. You are to return to the file an index card on *Barry C. Wayne Materials and Supplies Co.*
Of the following, the CORRECT alphabetical group that you should return the index card to is
   A. A to G   B. H to M   C. N to S   D. T to Z

4.____

Questions 5-10.

DIRECTIONS: In each of Questions 5 through 10, the names of four people are given. For each question, choose as your answer the one of the four names given which should be filed FIRST according to the usual system of alphabetical filing of names, as described in the following paragraph.

    In filing names, you must start with the last name. Names are filed in order of the first letter of the last name, then the second letter, etc. Therefore, BAILY would be filed before BROWN, which would be filed before COLT. A name with fewer letters of the same type comes first, i.e., Smith before Smithe. If the last names are the same, the names are filed alphabetically by the first name. If the first name is an initial, a name with an initial would come before a first name that starts with the same letter as the initial. Therefore, I. BROWN would come before IRA BROWN. Finally, if both last name and first name are the same, the name would be filed alphabetically by the middle name, once again an initial coming before a middle name which starts with the same letter as the initial. If there is no middle name at all, the name would come before those with middle initials or names.

SAMPLE QUESTION:
   A. Lester Daniels
   B. William Dancer
   C. Nathan Danzig
   D. Dan Lester

    The last names beginning with D are filed before the last name beginning with L. Since DANIELS, DANCER, and DANZIG all begin with the same three letters, you must look at the fourth letter of the last name to determine which name should be filed first. C comes before I or Z in the alphabet, so DANCER is filed before DANIELS or DANZIG. Therefore, the answer to the above sample question is B.

5.   A. Scott Biala
       B. Mary Byala
       C. Martin Baylor
       D. Francis Bauer

5.____

6.   A. Howard J. Black
       B. Howard Black
       C. J. Howard Black
       D. John H. Black

6.____

7.   A. Theodora Garth Kingston
       B. Theadore Barth Kingston
       C. Thomas Kingston
       D. Thomas T. Kingston

7.____

8. A. Paulette Mary Huerta
    B. Paul M. Huerta
    C. Paulette L. Huerta
    D. Peter A. Huerta

9. A. Martha Hunt Morgan
    B. Martin Hunt Morgan
    C. Mary H. Morgan
    D. Martine H. Morgan

10. A. James T. Meerschaum
    B. James M. Mershum
    C. James F. Mearshaum
    D. James N. Meshum

Questions 11-14.

DIRECTIONS: Questions 11 through 14 are to be answered SOLELY on the basis of the following information.

You are required to file various documents in file drawers which are labeled according to the following pattern:

DOCUMENTS

MEMOS		LETTERS	
File	Subject	File	Subject
84PM1	(A-L)	84PC1	(A-L)
84PM2	(M-Z)	84PC2	(M-Z)

REPORTS		INQUIRIES	
File	Subject	File	Subject
84PR1	(A-L)	84PQ1	(A-L)
84PR2	(M-Z)	84PQ2	(M-Z)

11. A letter dealing with a burglary should be filed in the drawer labeled
    A. 84PM1   B. 84PC1   C. 84PR1   D. 84PQ2

12. A report on Statistics should be found in the drawer labeled
    A. 84PM1   B. 84PC2   C. 84PR2   D. 84PQS

13. An inquiry is received about parade permit procedures. It should be filed in the drawer labeled
    A. 84PM2   B. 84PC1   C. 84PR1   D. 84PQ2

14. A police officer has a question about a robbery report you filed. You should pull this file from the drawer labeled
    A. 84PM1   B. 84PM2   C. 84PR1   D. 84PR2

Questions 15-22.

DIRECTIONS: Each of Questions 15 through 22 consists of four or six numbered names. For each question, choose the option (A, B, C, or D) which indicates the order in which the names should be filed in accordance with the following filing instructions:
- File alphabetically according to last name, then first name, then middle initial.
- File according to each successive letter within a name.
- When comparing two names in which the letters in the longer name are identical to the corresponding letters in the shorter name, the shorter name is filed first.
- When the last names are the same, initials are always filed before names beginning with the same letter.

15. I. Ralph Robinson
    II. Alfred Ross
    III. Luis Robles
    IV. James Roberts

    The CORRECT filing sequence for the above names should be
    A. IV, II, I, III   B. I, IV, III, II   C. III, IV, I, II   D. IV, I, III, II

16. I. Irwin Goodwin
    II. Inez Gonzalez
    III. Irene Goodman
    IV. Ira S. Goodwin
    V. Ruth I. Goldstein
    VI. M.B. Goodman

    The CORRECT filing sequence for the above names should be
    A. V, II, I, IV, III, VI   B. V, II, VI, III, IV, I
    C. V, II, III, VI, IV, I   D. V, II, III, VI, I, IV

17. I. George Allan
    II. Gregory Allen
    III. Gary Allen
    IV. George Allen

    The CORRECT filing sequence for the above names should be
    A. IV, III, I, II   B. I, IV, II, III   C. III, IV, I, II   D. I, III, IV, II

5 (#1)

18. I. Simon Kauffman
     II. Leo Kaufman
     III. Robert Kaufmann
     IV. Paul Kauffmann

     The CORRECT filing sequence for the above names should be
     A. I, IV, II, III   B. II, IV, III, I   C. III, II, IV, I   D. I, II, III, IV

19. I. Roberta Williams
     II. Robin Wilson
     III. Roberta Wilson
     IV. Robin Williams

     The CORRECT filing sequence for the above names should be
     A. III, II, IV, I   B. I, IV, III, II   C. I, II, III, IV   D. III, I, II, IV

20. I. Lawrence Shultz
     II. Albert Schultz
     III. Theodore Schwartz
     IV. Thomas Schwarz
     V. Alvin Schultz
     VI. Leonard Shultz

     The CORRECT filing sequence for the above names should be
     A. II, V, III, IV, I, VI   B. IV, III, V, I, II, VI
     C. II, V, I, VI, III, IV   D. I, VI, II, V, III, IV

21. I. McArdle
     II. Mayer
     III. Maletz
     IV. McNiff
     V. Meyer
     VI. MacMahon

     The CORRECT filing sequence for the above names should be
     A. I, IV, VI, III, II, V   B. II, I, IV, VI, III, V
     C. VI, III, II, I, IV, V   D. VI, III, II, V, I, IV

22. I. Jack E. Johnson
     II. R.H. Jackson
     III. Bertha Jackson
     IV. J.T. Johnson
     V. Ann Johns
     VI. John Jacobs

     The CORRECT filing sequence for the above names should be
     A. II, III, VI, V, IV, I   B. III, II, VI, V, IV, I
     C. VI, II, III, I, V, IV   D. III, II, VI, IV, V, I

Questions 23-30.

DIRECTIONS: The code table below shows 10 letters with matching numbers. For each question, there are three sets of letters. Each set of letters is followed by a set of numbers which may or may not match their correct letter according to the code table. For each question, check all three sets of letters and numbers and mark your answer:
  A. if no pairs are correctly matched
  B. if only one pair is correctly matched
  C. if only two pairs are correctly matched
  D. if all three pairs are correctly matched

CODE TABLE

T	M	V	D	S	P	R	G	B	H
1	2	3	4	5	6	7	8	9	0

SAMPLE QUESTION: TMVDSP – 123456
RGBHTM – 789011
DSPRGB – 256789

In the sample question above, the first set of numbers correctly match its set of letters. But the second and third pairs contain mistakes. In the second pair, M is correctly matched with number 1. According to the code table, letter M should be correctly matched with number 2. In the third pair, the letter D is incorrectly matched with number 2. According to the code table, letter D should be correctly matched with number 4. Since only one of the pairs is correctly matched, the answer to this sample question is B.

23. RSBMRM – 759262
    GDSRVH – 845730
    VDBRTM - 349713

24. TGVSDR – 183247
    SMHRDP – 520647
    TRMHSR - 172057

25. DSPRGM – 456782
    MVDBHT – 234902
    HPMDBT - 062491

26. BVPTRD – 936184
    GDPHMB – 807029
    GMRHMV - 827032

27. MGVRSH – 283750
    TRDMBS – 174295
    SPRMGV - 567283

28. SGBSDM – 489542   28.____
    MGHPTM – 290612
    MPBMHT - 269301

29. TDPBHM – 146902   29.____
    VPBMRS – 369275
    GDMBHM - 842902

30. MVPTBV – 236194   30.____
    PDRTMB – 47128
    BGTMSM - 981232

KEY (CORRECT ANSWERS)

1.	A	11.	B	21.	C		
2.	C	12.	C	22.	B		
3.	B	13.	D	23.	B		
4.	D	14.	D	24.	B		
5.	D	15.	D	25.	C		
6.	B	16.	C	26.	A		
7.	B	17.	D	27.	D		
8.	B	18.	A	28.	A		
9.	A	19.	B	29.	D		
10.	C	20.	A	30.	A		

TEST 2

DIRECTIONS: Each question or incomplete statement is followed by several suggested answers or completions. Select the one that BEST answers the question or completes the statement. *PRINT THE LETTER OF THE CORRECT ANSWER IN THE SPACE AT THE RIGHT.*

Questions 1-10.

DIRECTIONS: Questions 1 through 10 each consists of two columns, each containing four lines of names, numbers and/or addresses. For each question, compare the lines in Column I with the lines in Column II to see if they match exactly, and mark your answer A, B, C, or D, according to the following instructions:
- A. all four lines match exactly
- B. only three lines match exactly
- C. only two lines match exactly
- D. only one line matches exactly

COLUMN I | COLUMN II

1.
   I. Earl Hodgson — Earl Hodgson
   II. 1409870 — 1408970
   III. Shore Ave. — Schore Ave.
   IV. Macon Rd. — Macon Rd.

2.
   I. 9671485 — 9671485
   II. 470 Astor Court — 470 Astor Court
   III. Halprin, Phillip — Halperin, Phillip
   IV. Frank D. Poliseo — Frank D. Poliseo

3.
   I. Tandem Associates — Tandom Associates
   II. 144-17 Northern Blvd. — 144-17 Northern Blvd.
   III. Alberta Forchi — Albert Forchi
   IV. Kings Park, NY 10751 — Kings Point, NY 10751

4.
   I. Bertha C. McCormack — Bertha C. McCormack
   II. Clayton, MO — Clayton, MO
   III. 976-4242 — 976-4242
   IV. New City, NY 10951 — New City, NY 10951

5.
   I. George C. Morill — George C. Morrill
   II. Columbia, SC 29201 — Columbia, SD 29201
   III. Louis Ingham — Louis Ingham
   IV. 3406 Forest Ave. — 3406 Forest Ave.

6.
   I. 506 S. Elliott Pl. — 506 S. Elliott Pl.
   II. Herbert Hall — Hurbert Hall
   III. 4712 Rockaway Pkway — 4712 Rockaway Pkway
   IV. 169 E. 7 St. — 169 E. 7 St.

2 (#2)

7. I.   345 Park Ave.   345 Park Pl.   7._____
    II. Colman Oven Corp.   Coleman Oven Corp.
    III. Robert Conte   Robert Conti
    IV. 6179846   6179846

8. I.   Grigori Schierber   Grigori Schierber   8._____
    II. Des Moines, Iowa   Des Moines, Iowa
    III. Gouverneur Hospital   Gouverneur Hospital
    IV. 91-35 Cresskill Pl.   91-35 Cresskill Pl.

9. I.   Jeffery Janssen   Jeffrey Janssen   9._____
    II. 8041071   8041071
    III. 40 Rockefeller Plaza   40 Rockafeller Plaza
    IV. 407 6 St.   406 7 St.

10. I.   5971996   5871996   10._____
    II. 3113 Knickerbocker Ave. 31123 Knickerbocker Ave.
    III. 8434 Boston Post Rd.   8424 Boston Post Rd.
    IV. Penn Station   Penn Station

Questions 11-14.

DIRECTIONS: Questions 11 through 14 are to be answered by looking at the four groups of names and addresses listed below (I, II, III, and IV), and then finding out the number of groups that have their corresponding numbered lies exactly the same.

	GROUP I	GROUP II
Line 1.	Richmond General Hospital	Richman General Hospital
Line 2.	Geriatric Clinic	Geriatric Clinic
Line 3.	3975 Paerdegat St.	3975 Peardegat St.
Line 4.	Loudonville, New York 11538	Londonville, New York 11538

	GROUP III	GROUP IV
Line 1.	Richmond General Hospital	Richmend General Hospital
Line 2.	Geriatric Clinic	Geriatric Clinic
Line 3.	3795 Paerdegat St.	3975 Paerdegat St.
Line 4.	Loudonville, New York 11358	Loudonville, New York 11538

1. In how many groups is line one exactly the same?   11._____
    A. Two   B. Three   C. Four   D. None

12. In how many groups is line two exactly the same?   12._____
    A. Two   B. Three   C. Four   D. None

13. In how many groups is line three exactly the same?   13._____
    A. Two   B. Three   C. Four   D. None

14. In how many groups is line four exactly the same?   14.____
    A. Two   B. Three   C. Four   D. None

Questions 15-18.

DIRECTIONS: Each of Questions 15 through 18 has two lists of names and addresses. Each list contains three sets of names and addresses. Check each of the three sets in the list on the right to see if they are the same as the corresponding set in the list on the left. Mark your answers:
    A. if none of the sets in the right list are the same as those in the left list
    B. if only one of the sets in the right list is the same as those in the left list
    C. if only two of the sets in the right list are the same as those in the left list
    D. if all three sets in the right list are the same as those in the left list

15. Mary T. Berlinger   Mary T. Berlinger   15.____
    2351 Hampton St.   2351 Hampton St.
    Monsey, N.Y. 20117   Monsey, N.Y. 20117

    Eduardo Benes   Eduardo Benes
    483 Kingston Avenue   473 Kingston Avenue
    Central Islip, N.Y. 11734   Central Islip, N.Y. 11734

    Alan Carrington Fuchs   Alan Carrington Fuchs
    17 Gnarled Hollow Road   17 Gnarled Hollow Road
    Los Angeles, CA 91635   Los Angeles, CA 91685

16. David John Jacobson   David John Jacobson   16.____
    178 34 St. Apt. 4C   178 53 St. Apt. 4C
    New York, N.Y. 00927   New York, N.Y. 00927

    Ann-Marie Calonella   Ann-Marie Calonella
    7243 South Ridge Blvd.   7243 South Ridge Blvd.
    Bakersfield, CA 96714   Bakersfield, CA 96714

    Pauline M. Thompson   Pauline M. Thomson
    872 Linden Ave.   872 Linden Ave.
    Houston, Texas 70321   Houston, Texas 70321

17. Chester LeRoy Masterton   Chester LeRoy Masterson   17.____
    152 Lacy Rd.   152 Lacy Rd.
    Kankakee, Ill. 54532   Kankakee, Ill. 54532

    William Maloney   William Maloney
    S. LaCrosse Pla.   S. LaCross Pla.
    Wausau, Wisconsin 52136   Wausau, Wisconsin 52146

    Cynthia V. Barnes   Cynthia V. Barnes
    16 Pines Rd.   16 Pines Rd.
    Greenpoint, Miss. 20376   Greenpoint,, Miss. 20376

4 (#2)

18. Marcel Jean Frontenac   Marcel Jean Frontenac   18.____
    8 Burton On The Water   6 Burton On The Water
    Calender, Me. 01471   Calender, Me. 01471

    J. Scott Marsden   J. Scott Marsden
    174 S. Tipton St.   174 Tipton St.
    Cleveland, Ohio   Cleveland, Ohio

    Lawrence T. Haney   Lawrence T. Haney
    171 McDonough St.   171 McDonough St.
    Decatur, Ga. 31304   Decatur, Ga. 31304

Questions 19-26.

DIRECTIONS: Each of Questions 19 through 26 has two lists of numbers. Each list contains three sets of numbers. Check each of the three sets in the list on the right to see if they are the same as the corresponding set in the list on the left. Mark your answers:
- A. if none of the sets in the right list are the same as those in the left list
- B. if only one of the sets in the right list is the same as those in the left list
- C. if only two of the sets in the right list are the same as those in the left list
- D. if all three sets in the right list are the same as those in the left lists

19. 7354183476   7354983476   19.____
    4474747744   4474747774
    5791430231   57914302311

20. 7143592185   7143892185   20.____
    8344517699   8344518699
    9178531263   9178531263

21. 2572114731   257214731   21.____
    8806835476   8806835476
    8255831246   8255831246

22. 331476853821   331476858621   22.____
    6976658532996   6976655832996
    3766042113715   3766042113745

23. 8806663315   88066633115   23.____
    74477138449   74477138449
    211756663666   211756663666

24. 990006966996   99000696996   24.____
     53022219743   53022219843
     4171171117717   4171171177717

25. 24400222433004   24400222433004   25.____
     5300030055000355   5300030055500355
     20000075532002022   20000075532002022

26. 61116664066001116   61116664066001116   26.____
     7111300117001100733 7111300117001100733
     26666446664476518   26666446664476518

Questions 27-30.

DIRECTIONS: Questions 27 through 30 are to be answered by picking the answer which is in the correct numerical order, from the lowest number to the highest number, in each question.

27. A. 44533, 44518, 44516, 44547   27.____
     B. 44516, 44518, 44533, 44547
     C. 44547, 44533, 44518, 44516
     D. 44518, 44516, 44547, 44533

28. A. 95587, 95593, 95601, 95620   28.____
     B. 95601, 95620, 95587, 95593
     C. 95593, 95587, 95601. 95620
     D. 95620, 95601, 95593, 95587

29. A. 232212, 232208, 232232, 232223   29.____
     B. 232208, 232223, 232212, 232232
     C. 232208, 232212, 232223, 232232
     D. 232223, 232232, 232208, 232208

30. A. 113419, 113521, 113462, 113462   30.____
     B. 113588, 113462, 113521, 113419
     C. 113521, 113588, 113419, 113462
     D. 113419, 113462, 113521, 113588

KEY (CORRECT ANSWERS)

1.	C	11.	A	21.	C
2.	B	12.	C	22.	A
3.	D	13.	A	23.	D
4.	A	14.	A	24.	A
5.	C	15.	C	25.	C
6.	B	16.	B	26.	C
7.	D	17.	B	27.	B
8.	A	18.	B	28.	A
9.	D	19.	B	29.	C
10.	C	20.	B	30.	D

NAME AND NUMBER COMPARISONS

COMMENTARY

This test seeks to measure your ability and disposition to do a job carefully and accurately, your attention to exactness and preciseness of detail, your alertness and versatility in discerning similarities and differences between things, and your power in systematically handling written language symbols.

It is actually a test of your ability to do academic and/or clerical work, using the basic elements of verbal (qualitative) and mathematical (quantitative) learning—words and numbers.

EXAMINATION SECTION

TEST 1

DIRECTIONS: Questions 1 through 6 consist of sets of names and addresses. In each question, the name and address in Column II should be an exact copy of the name and address in Column II. *PRINT IN THE SPACE AT THE RIGHT THE LETTER*
   A. if there is a mistake only in the name
   B. if there is a mistake only in the address
   C. if there is a mistake in both name and address
   D. If there is no mistake in either name or address

SAMPLE:
Michael Filbert   Michael Filbert
456 Reade Street   644 Reade Street
New York, N.Y. 10013   New York, N.Y. 10013

Since there is a mistake only in the address, the answer is B.

1. Esta Wong   Esta Wang   1.____
   141 West 68 St.   141 West 68 St.
   New York, N.Y. 10023   New York, N.Y. 10023

2. Dr. Alberto Grosso   Dr. Alberto Grosso   2.____
   3475 12th Avenue   3475 12th Avenue
   Brooklyn, N.Y. 11218   Brooklyn, N.Y. 11218

3. Mrs. Ruth Bortlas   Ms. Ruth Bortias   3.____
   482 Theresa Ct.   482 Theresa Ct.
   Far Rockaway, N.Y. 11691 Far Rockaway, N.Y. 11169

4. Mr. and Mrs. Howard Fox   Mr. and Mrs. Howard Fox   4.____
   2301 Sedgwick Ave.   231 Sedgwick Ave.
   Bronx, N.Y. 10468   Bronx, N.Y. 10468

5. Miss Marjorie Black   Miss Margorie Black   5.____
   223 East 23 Street   223 East 23 Street
   New York, N.Y. 10010   New York, N.Y. 10010

2 (#1)

6. Michelle Herman   Michelle Hermann   6._____
   806 Valley Rd.   806 Valley Dr.
   Old Tappan, N.J. 07675 Old Tappan, N.J. 07675

KEY (CORRECT ANSWERS)

1. A
2. D
3. C
4. B
5. A
6. C

TEST 2

DIRECTIONS: Questions 1 through 6 consist of sets of names and addresses. In each question, the name and address in Column II should be an exact copy of the name and address in Column II. *PRINT IN THE SPACE AT THE RIGHT THE LETTER*
- A. if there is a mistake only in the name
- B. if there is a mistake only in the address
- C. if there is a mistake in both name and address
- D. If there is no mistake in either name or address

1. Ms. Joan Kelly
   313 Franklin Ave.
   Brooklyn, N.Y. 11202

   Ms. Joan Kielly
   318 Franklin Ave.
   Brooklyn, N.Y. 11202

   1.____

2. Mrs. Eileen Engel
   47-24 86 Road
   Queens, N.Y. 11122

   Mrs. Ellen Engel
   47-24 86 Road
   Queens, N.Y. 11122

   2.____

3. Marcia Michaels
   213 E. 81 St.
   New York, N.Y. 10012

   Marcia Michaels
   213 E. 81 St.
   New York, N.Y. 10012

   3.____

4. Rev. Edward J. Smyth
   1401 Brandeis Street
   San Francisco, Calif. 96201

   Rev. Edward J. Smyth
   1401 Brandies Street
   San Francisco, Calif. 96201

   4.____

5. Alicia Rodriguez
   24-68 81 St.
   Elmhurst, N.Y. 11122

   Alicia Rodriquez
   2468 81 St.
   Elmhurst, N.Y. 11122

   5.____

6. Ernest Eissemann
   21 Columbia St.
   New York, N.Y. 10007

   Ernest Eisermann
   21 Columbia St.
   New York, N.Y. 10007

   6.____

KEY (CORRECT ANSWERS)

1. C
2. A
3. D
4. B
5. C
6. A

TEST 3

DIRECTIONS: Questions 1 through 8 consist of names, locations, and telephone numbers. In each question, the name, location and number in Column II should be an exact copy of the name, location, and number in Column I. *PRINT IN THE SPACE AT THE RIGHT THE LETTER*
- A. if there is a mistake in one line only
- B. if there is a mistake in two lines only
- C. if there is a mistake in three lines only
- D. if there are no mistakes in any of the lines

1. Ruth Lang
   EAM Bldg., Room C101
   625-2000, ext. 765

   Ruth Lang
   EAM Bldg., Room C110
   625-2000, ext. 765

   1._____

2. Anne Marie Ionozzi
   Investigations, Room 827
   576-4000, ext. 832

   Anna Marie Ionozzi
   Investigation, Room 827
   566-4000, ext. 832

   2._____

3. Willard Jameson
   Fm C Bldg. Room 687
   454-3010

   Willard Jamieson
   Fm C Bldg. Room 687
   454-3010

   3._____

4. Joanne Zimmermann
   Bldg. SW, Room 314
   532-4601

   Joanne Zimmermann
   Bldg. SW, Room 314
   532-4601

   4._____

5. Carlyle Whetstone
   Payroll Division-A, Room 212A
   262-5000, ext. 471

   Caryle Whetstone
   Payroll Division-A, Room 212A
   262-5000, ext. 417

   5._____

6. Kenneth Chiang
   Legal Council, Room 9745
   (201) 416-9100, ext. 17

   Kenneth Chiang
   Legal Counsel, Room 9745
   (201) 416-9100, ext. 17

   6._____

7. Ethel Koenig
   Personnel Services Div, Rm 433
   635-7572

   Ethel Hoenig
   Personal Services Div, Rm 433
   635-7527

   7._____

8. Joyce Ehrhardt
   Office of Administrator, Rm W56
   387-8706

   Joyce Ehrhart
   Office of Administrator, Rm W56
   387-7806

   8._____

KEY (CORRECT ANSWERS)

1. A
2. C
3. A
4. D
5. B
6. A
7. C
8. B

TEST 4

DIRECTIONS: Each of Questions 1 through 10 gives the identification number and name of a person who has received treatment at a certain hospital. You are to choose the option (A, B, C, or D) which has EXACTLY the same number and name as those given in the question.

SAMPLE QUESTION:
123765 Frank Y. Jones
- A. 123675 Frank Y. Jones
- B. 123765 Frank T. Jones
- C. 123765 Frank Y. Jones
- D. 123765 Frank Y. Jones

The correct answer is D, because it is the only option showing the identification number and name exactly as they are in the sample question.

1. 754898 Diane Malloy
   - A. 745898 Diane Malloy
   - B. 754898 Dion Malloy
   - C. 754898 Diane Malloy
   - D. 754898 Diane Maloy

2. 661818 Ferdinand Figueroa
   - A. 661818 Ferdinand Figeuroa
   - B. 661618 Ferdinand Figueroa
   - C. 661818 Ferdnand Figueroa
   - D. 661818 Ferdinand Figueroa

3. 100101 Norman D. Braustein
   - A. 100101 Norman D. Braustein
   - B. 101001 Norman D. Braustein
   - C. 100101 Norman P. Braustien
   - D. 100101 Norman D. Bruastein

4. 838696 Robert Kittredge
   - A. 838969 Robert Kittredge
   - B. 838696 Robert Kittredge
   - C. 388696 Robert Kittredge
   - D. 838696 Robert Kittridge

5. 243716 Abraham Soletsky
   - A. 243716 Abrahm Soletsky
   - B. 243716 Abraham Solestky
   - C. 243176 Abraham Soletsky
   - D. 243716 Abraham Soletsky

6. 981121 Phillip M. Maas
   - A. 981121 Phillip M. Mass
   - B. 981211 Phillip M. Maas
   - C. 981121 Phillip M. Maas
   - D. 981121 Phillip N. Maas

7. 786556 George Macalusso
   - A. 785656 George Macalusso
   - B. 786556 George Macalusso
   - C. 786556 George Maculusso
   - D. 786556 George Macluasso

8. 639472 Eugene Weber
   - A. 639472 Eugene Weber
   - B. 639472 Eugene Webre
   - C. 693472 Eugene Weber
   - D. 639742 Eugene Weber

2 (#4)

9. 724936 John J. Lomonaco 9.____
    A. 724936 John J. Lomanoco   B. 724396 John L. Lomonaco
    C. 7224936 John J. Lomonaco   D. 724936 John J. Lamonaco

10. 899868 Michael Schnitzer 10.____
    A. 899868 Micheal Schnitzer   B. 898968 Michael Schnizter
    C. 899688 Michael Schnitzer   D. 899868 Michael Schnitzer

KEY (CORRECT ANSWERS)

1.	C	6.	C
2.	D	7.	B
3.	A	8.	A
4.	B	9.	C
5.	D	10.	D

NAME AND NUMBER CHECKING
EXAMINATION SECTION
TEST 1

DIRECTIONS: This test is designed to measure your speed/and accuracy. You are urged to work both quickly and accurately and to do correctly as many lists as you can in the time allowed. The test consists of lists or pairs of names and numbers. Count the number of IDENTICAL pairs in each list. Then, select the correct number, 1, 2, 3, 4, 5, and indicate your choice in the space at the right. Two sample questions are presented for your guidance, together with the correct solutions.

SAMPLE LIST A
Adelphi College   – Adelphia College
Braxton Corp   – Braxeton Corp.
Wassaic State School   – Wassaic State School
Central Islip State Hospital – Central Isllip State Hospital
Greenwich House   – Greenwich House

NOTE: There are only two correct pairs—Wassaic State School and Greenwich House. Therefore, the CORRECT answer is 2.

SAMPLE LIST B
78453694   – 78453684
784530   – 784530
533   – 534
67845   – 67845
2368745   – 2368755

NOTE: There are only two correct pairs—784530 and 67845. Therefore, the CORRECT answer is 2.

LIST 1   1.____
    98654327   - 98654327
    74932564   - 7492564
    61438652   - 61438652
    01297653   - 01287653
    1865439765   - 1865439765

LIST 2   2.____
    478362   - 478363
    278354792   - 278354772
    9327   - 9327
    297384625   - 27384625
    6428156   - 6428158

LIST 3
Abbey House — - Abbey House
Actor's Fund Home — - Actor's Fund Home
Adrian Memorial — - Adrian Memorial
A. Clayton Powell Home — - Clayton Powell House
Abbot E. Kittredge Club — - Abbott E. Kitteredge Club

3.____

LIST 4
3682 — - 3692
21937453829 — - 31927453829
723 — - 733
2763920 — - 2763920
47293 — - 47293

4.____

LIST 5
Adra House — - Adra House
Adolescents' Court — - Adolescents' Court
Cliff Villa — - Cliff Villa
Clark Neighborhood House — - Clark Neighborhood House
Alma Mathews House — - Alma Mathews House

5.____

LIST 6
28734291 — - 28734271
63810263849 — - 63810263846
26831027 — - 26831027
368291 — - 368291
7238102637 — - 7238102637

6.____

LIST 7
Albion State T.S. — - Albion State T.C.
Clara de Hirsch Home — - Clara De Hirsch Home
Alice Carrington Royce — - Alice Carington Royce
Alice Chopin Nursery — - Alice Chapin Nursery
Lighthouse Eye Clinic — - Lighthouse Eye Clinic

7.____

LIST 8
327 — - 329
712438291026 — - 712438291026
2753829142 — - 275382942
826287 — - 826289
26435162839 — - 26435162839

8.____

LIST 9
Letchworth Village — - Letchworth Village
A.A.A.E. Inc. — - A.A.A.E. Inc.
Clear Pool Camp — - Clear Pool Camp
A.M.M.L.A. Inc. — - A.M.M.L.A. Inc.
J.G. Harbard — - J.G. Harbord

9.____

3 (#1)

LIST 10   10.____
- 8254 — 8256
- 2641526 — 2641526
- 4126389012 — 4126389102
- 725 — 725
- 76253917287 — 76253917287

LIST 11   11.____
- Attica State Prison — Attica State Prison
- Nellie Murrah — Nellie Murrah
- Club Marshall — Club Marshal
- Assissium Casea-Maria — Assissium Casa-Maria
- The Homestead — The Homestead

LIST 12   12.____
- 2691 — 2691
- 623819253627 — 623819253629
- 28637 — 28937
- 278392736 — 278392736
- 52739 — 52739

LIST 13   13.____
- A.I.C.P. Boys Camp — A.I.C.P. Boy's Camp
- Einar Chrystie — Einar Christyie
- Astoria Center — Astoria Center
- G. Frederick Brown — G. Federick Browne
- Vacation Service — Vacation Services

LIST 14   14.____
- 728352689 — 728352688
- 643728 — 643728
- 37829176 — 37827196
- 8425367 — 8425369
- 65382018 — 65382018

LIST 15   15.____
- E.S. Streim — E.S. Strim
- Charles E. Higgins — Charles E. Higgins
- Baluvelt, N.Y. — Blauwelt, N.Y.
- Roberta Magdalen — Roberto Magdalen
- Ballard School — Ballard School

LIST 16   16.____
- 7382 — 7392
- 281374538299 — 291374538299
- 623 — 633
- 6273730 — 6273730
- 63392 — 63392

LIST 17
    Orrin Otis   - Orrin Otis
    Barat Settlement   - Barat Settlemen
    Emmanuel House   - Emmanuel House
    William T. McCreery   - William T. McCreery
    Seamen's Home   - Seaman's Home

17.____

LIST 18
    72824391   - 72834371
    3729106237   - 37291106237
    82620163849   - 82620163846
    37638921   - 37638921
    82631027   - 82631027

18.____

LIST 19
    Commonwealth Fund   - Commonwealth Fund
    Anne Johnsen   - Anne Johnson
    Bide-A-Wee Home   - Bide-a-Wee Home
    Riverdale-on-Hudson   - Riverdal-on-Hudson
    Bialystoker Home   - Bailystoker Home

19.____

LIST 20
    9271   - 9271
    392918352627   - 392018852629
    72637   - 72637
    927392736   - 927392736
    92739   - 92739

20.____

LIST 21
    Charles M. Stump   - Charles M. Stump
    Bourne Workshop   - Buorne Workshop
    B'nai Bi'rith   - B'nai Brith
    Poppenhuesen Institute   - Poppenhuesen Institute
    Consular Service   - Consular Service

21.____

LIST 22
    927352689   - 927352688
    647382   - 648382
    93729176   - 93727196
    649536718   - 649536718
    5835367   - 5835369

22.____

LIST 23
    L.S. Bestend   - L.S. Bestent
    Hirsch Mfg. Co.   - Hircsh Mfg. Co.
    F.H. Storrs   - F.P. Storrs
    Camp Wassaic   - Camp Wassaic
    George Ballingham   - George Ballingham

23.____

5 (#1)

LIST 24
    372846392048   - 372846392048
    334   - 334
    7283524678   - 7283524678
    7283   - 7283
    7283629372   - 7283629372

24.____

LIST 25
    Dr. Stiles Company   - Dr. Stills Company
    Frances Hunsdon   - Frances Hunsdon
    Northrop Barrert   - Nothrup Barrent
    J.D. Brunjes   - J.D. Brunjes
    Theo. Claudel & Co.   - Theo. Claudel co.

25.____

KEY (CORRECT ANSWERS)

1.	3	11.	3
2.	1	12.	3
3.	2	13.	1
4.	2	14.	2
5.	5	15.	2
6.	3	16.	2
7.	1	17.	3
8.	2	18.	2
9.	4	19.	2
10.	3	20.	4

21.	2
22.	1
23.	2
24.	5
25.	2

TEST 2

DIRECTIONS: This test is designed to measure your speed/and accuracy. You are urged to work both quickly and accurately and to do correctly as many lists as you can in the time allowed. The test consists of lists or pairs of names and numbers. Count the number of IDENTICAL pairs in each list. Then, select the correct number, 1, 2, 3, 4, 5, and indicate your choice in the space at the right.

LIST 1   1.____
    82728   - 82738
    82736292637   - 82736292639
    728   - 738
    83926192527   - 83726192529
    82736272   - 82736272

LIST 2   2.____
    L. Pietri   - L. Pietri
    Mathewson, L.F.   - Mathewson, L.F.
    Funk & Wagnall   - Funk & Wagnalls
    Shimizu, Sojio   - Shimizu, Sojio
    Filing Equipment Bureau - Filing Equipment Buraeu

LIST 3   3.____
    63801829374   - 63801839474
    283577657   - 283577657
    65689   - 65689
    3457892026   - 3547893026
    2779   - 2778

LIST 4   4.____
    August Caille   - August Caille
    The Well-Fare Service   - The Wel-Fare Service
    K.L.M. Process co.   - R.L.M. Process Co.
    Merrill Littell   - Merrill Littell
    Dodd & Sons   - Dodd & Son

LIST 5   5.____
    998745732   - 998745733
    723   - 723
    463849102983   - 463849102983
    8570   - 8570
    279012   - 279012

LIST 6   6.____
    M.A. Wender   - M.A. Winder
    Minneapolis Supply Co.   - Minneapolis Supply Co.
    Beverly Hills Corp   - Beverley Hills Corp.
    Trafalgar Square   - Trafalgar Square
    Phifer, D.T.   - Phiefer, D.T.

LIST 7
    7834629   - 7834629
    3549806746   - 3549806746
    97802564   - 97892564
    689246   - 688246
    2578024683   - 2578024683

7.____

LIST 8
    Scadrons'   - Scadrons'
    Gensen & Bro.   - Genson & Bro.
    Firestone Co.   - Firestone Co.
    H.L. Eklund   - H.L. Eklund
    Oleomargarine Co.   - Oleomargarine Co.

8.____

LIST 9
    782039485618   - 782039485618
    53829172639   - 63829172639
    892   - 892
    82937482   - 829374820
    52937456   - 53937456

9.____

LIST 10
    First Nat'l Bank   - First Nat'l Bank
    Sedgwick Machine Works - Sedgewick Machine Works
    Hectographia Co.   - Hectographia Corp.
    Levet Bros.   - Levet Bros.
    Multistamp Co., Inc.   - Multistamp Co., Inc.

10.____

LIST 11
    7293   - 7293
    6382910293   - 6382910292
    981928374012   - 981928374912
    58293   - 58393
    18203649271   - 283019283745

11.____

LIST 12
    Lowrey Lb'r Co.   - Lowrey Lb'r Co.
    Fidelity Service   - Fidelity Service
    Reumann, J.A.   - Reumann, J.A.
    Duophoto Ltd.   - Duophotos Ltd.
    John Jarratt   - John Jaratt

12.____

LIST 13
    6820384   - 6820384
    383019283745   - 383019283745
    63927102   - 63928102
    91029354829   - 91029354829
    58291728   - 58291728

13.____

LIST 14   14.____
    Standard Press Co.   - Standard Press Co.
    Reliant Mf'g. Co.   - Relant Mf'g Co.
    M.C. Lynn   - M.C. Lynn
    J. Fredericks Company   - G. Fredericks Company
    Wandermann, B.S.   - Wanderman, B.S.

LIST 15   15.____
    4283910293   - 4283010203
    992018273648   - 992018273848
    620   - 629
    752937273   - 752937373
    5392   - 5392

LIST 16   16.____
    Waldorf Hotel   - Waldorf Hotel
    Aaron Machinery Co.   - Aaron Machinery Co.
    Caroline Ann Locke   - Caroline Ane Locke
    McCabe Mfg. Co.   - McCabe Mfg. Co.
    R.L. Landres   - R.L. Landers

LIST 17   17.____
    68391028364   - 68391028394
    68293   - 68293
    739201   - 739201
    72839201   - 72839211
    739917   - 739719

LIST 18   18.____
    Balsam M.M.   - Balsamm, M.M.
    Steinway & Co.   - Stienway & M. Co.
    Eugene Elliott   - Eugene A. Elliott
    Leonard Loan Co.   - Leonard Loan Co.
    Frederick Morgan   - Frederick Morgen

LIST 19   19.____
    8929   - 9820
    392836472829   - 392836572829
    462   - 4622039271
    827   - 2039276837
    53829   - 54829

LIST 20   20.____
    Danielson's Hofbrau   - Danielson's Hafbrau
    Edward A. Truarme   - Edward A. Truame
    Insulite Co.   - Insulite Co.
    Reisler Shoe Corp.   - Rielser Shoe Corp.
    L.L. Thompson   - L.L. Thompson

4 (#2)

LIST 21
    92839102837   - 92839102837
    58891028   - 58891028
    7291728   - 7291928
    272839102839   - 272839102839
    428192   - 428102

21.____

LIST 22
    K.L. Veiller   - K.L. Veiller
    Webster, Roy   - Webster, Ray
    Drasner Spring Co.   - Drasner Spring Co.
    Edward J. Cravenport   - Edward J. Cravanport
    Harold Field   - Harold A. Field

22.____

LIST 23
    2293   - 2293
    4283910293   - 5382910292
    871928374012   - 871928374912
    68293   - 68393
    8120364927   - 81293649271

23.____

LIST 24
    Tappe, Inc   - Tappe, Inc.
    A.M. Wentingworth   - A.M. Wentinworth
    Scott A. Elliott   - Scott A. Elliott
    Echeverria Corp.   - Echeverria Corp.
    Bradford Victor Company   - Bradford Victer Company

24.____

LIST 25
    4820384   - 4820384
    393019283745   - 283919283745
    63917102   - 63927102
    91029354829   - 91029354829
    48291728   - 48291728

25.____

KEY (CORRECT ANSWERS)

1.	1	11.	1
2.	3	12.	3
3.	2	13.	4
4.	2	14.	2
5.	4	15.	1
6.	2	16.	3
7.	3	17.	2
8.	4	18.	1
9.	2	19.	1
10.	3	20.	2

21. 3
22. 2
23. 1
24. 2
25. 4

www.ingramcontent.com/pod-product-compliance
Lightning Source LLC
Chambersburg PA
CBHW080739230426
43665CB00020B/2790